CHAKA!

THROUGH THE FIRE

CHAKA KHAN

with Tonya Bolden

RODALE

COPYRIGHT PAGE

TK

In memory of Geneva "Pepsi" Charles (1948–2002),
print and broadcast journalist, youth and community
activist, and cherished friend.

ACKNOWLEDGMENTS

TK

CONTENTS

CONTENTS

EPIGRAPH

TK

PRELUDE

A lot of people think it's a miracle that I didn't wind up like Hendrix or Joplin. And whenever I've been asked why I didn't, I only have one answer.

"Hell if I know."

I don't mean to be flip. But that's a big question, don't you think? I find there's usually no neat, quick answer for those.

It seems to me that life is part chance, part plan, part a whole lot of other stuff we don't half understand. About the only thing I'm certain of is that my life has been a series of "happenings," that have made me who I am. Sometimes, you don't get the significance of a moment until much later. But sometimes it hits you full-on—as it did at the 2001 Essence Awards at Madison Square Garden.

That year, the honorees included Venus and Serena Williams, the Hageman Brothers for the school they created in Harlem, and Randall Robinson for his titan TransAfrica work. Sure, it's great to see good people get their props, but truth be told, I was in a pretty funky mood. Sometimes I hate show business, and that's what these awards shows tend to have way too much of. They can get pretty plastic. And by 2001, I was definitely into keeping it real.

As I made my way to my dressing room, I came to the green room. For a beat, I thought about hanging in there for a while. Lots of people. Lots of faces. Some I didn't know; most, familiar. But all I truly saw was people profiling, styling—all I heard was noise. Nah. The green room was *not* where I wanted to be. I headed on to my cubbyhole of a dressing room where Reggie and Mike would be ready to pounce: one to make my face; the other, my hair. (Hey, being beautiful takes work.)

My granddaughter was waiting for me. Just the sight of Raeven, in her perfect green chiffon gown, snapped me out of the blahs. Eight-year-old Raeven was my escort for the evening. What a quirky combo of lion and lamb—like me as a kid. Like me, still.

Will Raeven sing too? She sure has a voice.

Will Raeven give my daughter the hell I gave Mama?

At that moment, Raeven was a wonderful distraction from all the waiting—waiting in the dressing room, waiting in the audience . . . And I surprised myself by thinking, even briefly, about the future. As anyone who knows me would tell you, I'm an in-the-moment gal.

Thirty or so minutes before I was to go on, I left the audience and headed backstage. A seat-filler took my place—bald spots wouldn't do as long as the cameras were working the room.

Backstage, more waiting, and my mind roamed away. I was only half-watching the monitor when Samuel Jackson's better half, LaTonya Richardson, hit the stage and launched into this poem-like thing about children.

"... fifty thousand gone in just twelve years ..."

Say what?

The "blood of our children" LaTonya proclaimed, "the screams of fifty thousand."

I knew my spot followed a segment honoring women who had lost children to violence, but I had no idea this thing would get real, so close to the bone.

"Our communities are wasting into graveyards ... schools have become killing fields ... streets are strewn with spent clips." LaTonya took us all to task with a spin on "Word Up"— "So we just wave our hands in the air actin' like we *just don't care* ..."

Gang violence, school shootings, thousands of kids on Ritalin, too many parents too busy, and so many weak-ass schools. LaTonya was telling it straight—we're acting like we just don't care. Not enough of us give a fuck.

"America!" she screamed. "Fifty thousand ghost children rising up to indict us ..."

I was in tears, messing up much of Reggie's work, but I didn't care.

I took a deep breath and pulled myself together, only to well up again when Camille Cosby took the mike.

"I live with the loss . . . every day." Camille's words about Ennis's murder were dignified and few as she readied the audience for the video of Charlotte Austin Jordan, Dee Sumpter, Yvonne Pointer-Triplett, and Francis Davis recounting the nightmare they live with 24/7.

Charlotte's little girl had been AK-47'd to death in some insane L.A. street shit. Eight years later, Charlotte's son was gunned down.

Dee's daughter had been strangled by a serial killer in her home in Charlotte, North Carolina.

Yvonne's daughter had been raped, murdered, then dumped in an abandoned building not far from her home in Cleveland. That bright, beautiful child had been on her way to school to receive an award for perfect attendance.

Frances lost three sons—*all* of her children—within a span of six years. They'd been shot dead—practically in the same damn spot in Brooklyn.

As I listened to these horrible stories, it dawned on me that Mother's Day was about two weeks away. *How do these sisters brace themselves for that day, year after year?*

Talk about through the fire. They had done more than survive; they had truly prevailed, channeling their pain into something good: Dee, with Mothers of Murdered Offspring; Yvonne, with Positive Plus; Francis, with Mothers of All Children; and Charlotte, with Save Our Future.

"Four mothers reaching back," said the announcer, "divinely guided by the spirits of their lost children."

The women came out onto the stage to the strains of "The Greatest Love of All." I couldn't imagine a dry eye in the house. This was no longer a mere show.

People were on their feet, giving up praise, prayer—and gratitude—to these four Queens, ordinary sisters humbling every damn one of us "stars."

The applause sounded close to holy. We weren't cheering the women so much as we were hugging them, loving them, saying, *We're sorry—we're so, so sorry.* There was healing going on, blessings counted, one by one.

Shit. We have to sing after this?

"We" was Jennifer Holiday, Gladys Knight, and me.

As Dee, Charlotte, Francis, and Yvonne stood center stage, their mere presence challenged us all to do better by the children.

Yvonne was the last to speak. "I don't stand here in glory," she said, "I stand here between pain and joy."

Huge ovation as they left the stage. I was about to lose it again—and I was on in a few.

Breathe, Chaka, breathe.

Regal Gladys entered and took us into "Something Blue." I was feeling for her too: she had lost her son, Jimmy, not that long ago.

"There is something blue in my soul without you," she sang.

So much of Milini and Damien's growing up I missed out on. So many dramas and traumas I laid on them.

On a strength not my own, I walked out as Gladys sailed

into "Missing You." Jennifer joined us right after that.

I entered that zone, that merciful, boundless place of no walls, no glaring lights, nothing but pure light, pure life. I became all voice. Voice became all my love, hopes, prayers, every sorrow, and all my sorrys. I sang for the fifty thousand children, for every Dee, Charlotte, Francis, and Yvonne in the world.

I had my children still, and their children. I had my life still.

To Hell and Back in a Limousine. That was going to be the title of my memoir when I started working on it years ago with my friend Pepsi Charles. Later, *I'm Every Woman* was going to be the title. In interview after interview, when asked, "What are you working on?" there was usually a new CD in the works, and along with that I'd say "I'm working on my book!" Never happened. Why?

That's another one of those big questions. In part, I think I sabotaged the effort because I wasn't really ready to remember my mad mistakes, my dark nights of the soul, the loneliness, the losing myself not just in drugs and booze, but in my Wild Child act.

At the Essence Awards, I thought—hell, my torments don't compare with the sufferings of those fifty thousand children, or with the grief Charlotte, Dee, Yvonne, and Frances will have to endure for the rest of their lives.

It's not just about you, Chaka! My sister Tammy would remind me over the years, as I waffled on whether to tell my story or not. She was convinced she could have helped me help myself sooner if she had been able to read a story like mine when she was living in constant fear that I'd drug myself to death—

literally. *Maybe I could have helped you help yourself sooner, Chaka.*

On that night in April 2001, I finally felt truly ready to review my life: things I've done and things I've left undone. I also knew I'd have to take a good look at things I'd said over the years—on the fly, in a fury, when fatigued—that were half-truths, or not true at all. And I dared to start believing that perhaps my story could be a help, a lesson, in many cases on how NOT to live your life. If nothing else, I thought, perhaps I owed it to my grandchildren to leave a real record of myself.

1

BABY ME

Big Mama Thornton's "Hound Dog" is a huge hit. The killing in Korea is in year three. Vee Jay Records has opened up shop in the "I Will" city—and not far away, at the naval hospital in Great Lakes, Illinois, here I come after putting eighteen-year-old Sandra Naomi Sallie Page Stevens through thirty-nine hours of labor. March 23, '53.

I was a monkey wrench. When my mother got pregnant, she was in her first year of a teacher-prep program at what is today Chicago's Malcolm X College. She had a scholarship to the Art Institute. She most definitely had plans.

My mother was the daughter of strivers: Maude, out of Macon, Georgia; Elmer, Kansas City. The couple had worked hard, scrimping and saving to avoid ever renting again—to buy a home of their own: Maude worked days as a dietician for the Board of Ed.; Elmer worked nights as a soap factory foreman. Then, while training a recent hire, thirty-four-year old Elmer Page got electrocuted as he stood atop a wet grounded barrel.

Strong Maude became stronger to raise as best she could her two girls: my mother, nine; Barbara, eight.

The Page sisters spent most of their childhood Northside in the much ballyhooed multicultural experiment—Italian, Irish, Jewish, Asian, Polish, "Negro"—that was the Frances Cabrini Homes back in the early '40s.

Cabrini boasted neat green-doored, red-brick townhouse-type homes: a little back yard, a little front yard; government-issue coal delivered into the furnace room chute; short, clean streets, their names inscribed on totem poles. Cabrini was a step-up for working class folks. Cabrini-ites took pride in their homes, never imagining they would one day be dwarfed and blighted by the Cabrini Green high-rises.

Neighbors regarded the Pages as something close to rich, though they were far from it. Grandma Maude was simply a money-managing maven—making her children's clothes, buying food and household goods in bulk. That's why the Pages possessed the only telephone on their block for a long time and were among the first families in Cabrini to have a TV. Thanks to Maude's financial magic and great expectations, the Page sisters had the privilege of four years of pliés and pirouettes with the imperious Mrs. Sweifka, who couldn't be bothered with their first names—"Page 1, straighten the back! Page 2, right leg is incorrect!"

Years before the ballet lessons, the Page sisters had a taste of singing, when they attended Wayman African Methodist Episcopal Church with some neighbors for a time. Singing in the junior choir was the best part of the experience for them. Like some other kids, they sometimes teased the junior choir's pianist: slight, bespectacled Ramsey, who was in Aunt Barbara's class in elementary school. Practice! practice! practice! so often kept that boy out of the running when it came to having fun. Thank goodness he didn't give into peer pressure, for the world of jazz would be devoid of the brilliance of Ramsey Lewis.

It was in Cabrini that my mother met my father: Charles Stevens, aka Buddy. I don't know if his parents, Charles Alexander Stevens and Emily Marie Dennis, married in her Louisiana or his Arkansas, but after they did, they unwittingly became part of the Great Migration. In Chicago, Grandfather Charles found work with the Chicago & Northwestern.

Sandra Page was thirteen when she came down with a huge crush on Buddy (four years her senior), but she wasn't even a blip on his screen. Still, he stayed in her dreams even after he joined the Army Air Corps.

It would make nice copy to say the glory days of the Tuskegee Airmen had inspired my father, but going military was simply a lark. He was running the streets as a teenager, playing hooky with some friends, when a bet, boast, or dare led to his finagling a way to up his age and get into the service. He wound up stationed at Lackland, in San Antonio, Texas.

Cat-eyed Sandra was quite a looker by age sixteen. Home on furlough, Buddy finally took notice.

"He's too old for you!" objected Gramma Maude, but my mother paid her no mind, cuddling up with Buddy at the movies, in his mother's living room, or under starlight, whenever he was home on furlough. She penned long, love-drenched letters when he was back in Texas. Then, one day she found out her beloved was a bit of a trickster: what he called "furlough" the military called AWOL. (He was busted the day MPs came to claim him.)

It was after one of my father's "furloughs" that my mother's late period became no period at all.

For the longest time, I believed my mother had tried to abort me, which means, of course, that for the longest time, I thought I wasn't wanted. It's one thing to know you weren't planned. But unwanted? Try as I can, I can't remember what I thought I heard that led me to believe my mother had tried to abort me.

"Absolutely not!" That sums up my mother's response to that notion.

It was her doctor, who knew my mother had dreams, ambitions. And she wondered if he thought he was doing her a favor by poking her wrong, triggering blood from the womb.

"If you continue to bleed, you won't have this baby," he stated plainly.

He tried to abort my baby! My mother said she cried all the way home.

But baby me survived and that left Mama two options: bearing the stigma of being an unwed mother—remember this was in the '50s—or getting Buddy to "do the right thing." Either way, she'd have to quit college, put all her opportunities on hold. And so, she became Sandra Stevens when she was six months along with me.

She came to call me her "Miracle Child," not only because she thought the doctor tried to kill me, but because when I did finally exit the womb, I weighed just five pounds. Then, my mother had sleepless nights as I lay in an incubator: my weight had dipped to 4.6. My mother has said those two weeks away from me was pure torture. What relief and joy flooded her when she was finally able to bring home ME!: Yvette Marie. "Yvette" after the cool jazz tenor saxman Stan Getz tune. "Marie" after Daddy's mother (no one called her Emily).

We lived with Gramma Maude until my mother got her own apartment in Cabrini. Because she figured it was only a matter of time before my father went AWOL again, she decided to make the long train journey to Texas. Perhaps because I heard the story so often, or perhaps because some of the impossible is possible, I claim that journey as my earliest memory. I know you'll call me crazy, because I was only three months old when my father first laid eyes on me.

About a month later, Mama, Daddy and baby me were living together in Chicago. My father had opted for a dishonorable discharge rather than complete the few remaining months of his tour of duty. Turns out, I was just the first of their three kids. Yvonne Maude, aka Bonnie, was born eighteen months after me. Mark Elmer, in 1960.

Along the way, my father juggled a lot of jobs. He worked at several bookstores before he got a gig running a printing machine at the University of Chicago's National Opinion Research Center (NORC).

My mother made clothes for people, painted portraits, made jewelry, babysat, and did whatever else she could find to do, exploiting every talent, to help make ends meet. Some Mother's Days and Easters, she had Bonnie and me outside our apartment building on Ingleside in Hyde Park, selling paper flowers she had made to passersby en route to church. Some evenings and weekends—when it was crunchtime at NORC—she picked up extra money, collating questionnaires Daddy printed out.

For a while, my mother was the chief breadwinner, after my father broke an ankle. His boss had been good enough to give her a temporary job, as a collator. My mother would eventually work at NORC permanently for some eighteen years, rising from collator to field supervisor.

I'll never forget the day I stood broken-hearted at our living-room window, watching my mother, pregnant with Mark, riding her bike to work. I made a vow: "One day I'm going to buy my mother a house. I'm going to take care of her. "

If you did the math, we were poor, but I never felt poor or "deprived." My parents made life rich, extremely full. Both found an oasis in art. So wherever we lived—and we moved a lot— home was full of art. There were my father's charcoal sketches,

which my mother then oil painted. And she adorned our bedroom walls with murals and our favorite cartoon characters.
Whatever they couldn't afford—lamps, a living-room table—
they often built or recycled from something found. They both
had genius ways of making home a wonderland.

But home wasn't exactly a paradise. My parents fought;
they fought a lot, filling my early childhood with more than
enough drama.

I forgot all about those fights whenever I was with my father. He loved the outdoors. With him, everything was a great
adventure: the zoo, collecting leaves, long walks. He taught me
to handle a bow and arrow, and how to ride a bike. Some Saturdays, he'd take us to "The Point," the legendary peninsula of
a park that vees into Lake Michigan. Guys often formed im-
promptu bands at The Point, and I loved watching my father
get down on the congas.

And singing—my father was always singing, at The Point,
during a walk, around the house, any and everywhere else.
Many a night, when I was very young, he sang me to sleep with
some Nat King Cole, Sinatra, or B.B. King.

But many a night, I was later awakened by their fighting.
And it was my mother's great pleasure that was often their bone
of contention.

That woman *loved* to dance!—dance away worries about
rent-money and clothing the children and getting dinner done
and contending with her mercurial, sometimes inscrutable,
Buddy—who couldn't dance and couldn't *stand* her dancing.
Friday nights, Latin-style at Basin Street; Saturdays, a mix of

beats a block away, at Budland. My mother and Aunt Barbara were often at the clubs when the dancing commenced at nine, and they danced, and danced—they danced every dance—usually until the club closed at 4 A.M.

Mama was not stepping out on Daddy; she only wanted some dance-floor freedom, but he found that hard to believe. Time and again she told him she and Barbara wouldn't even let guys sit at their table. Time and again, she urged him to come out and at least *watch* her dance. They never had a problem finding a babysitter (not with Mama's clan around). But, no, my father's druthers was to stay home sipping wine or beer, playing chess, be-bopping to some Coltrane, Brubeck, Getz, Miles, and fuming, just spoiling for a fight.

"Where you been?" he asked, as he'd asked many a pre-dawn hour before.

"Dancing."

"With who?"

"Don't start again, Buddy. You know all about with who! Everyone!"

Mama was not up for fussing. "I'm sleepy."

"Well, you won't sleep yet—not till we have sex."

"Let me take a nap, okay?"

No rest for the weary.

He pushed, she shoved, she ran into the bathroom. He burst in and tried to drag her into their bedroom.

More pushing, shoving, shouting, tussling until she grabbed

a plaster bust and threatened to let it fly. (No mystery as to where I get my fire.)

When my father didn't back off, my mother kept her word. His blood ended up all over our beige couch, which she had recently reupholstered herself.

She called the cops. *Please just get him to leave me alone.*

The cops wanted to cut Daddy some slack, tried to coax him to collect himself, even offered to take him to a hospital. In response, Daddy started cussing out one of the cops. The next thing I knew, they were hauling him off.

I was ten, and terrified. I could have been twenty and I still would have been terrified. I vowed that when I grew up I'd never put my children through something like that.

I was used to my parents fighting, used to them making up, fighting, making up, and my father getting back to singing around the house. But not this time. Daddy wasn't just gone for a day; he was gone for good—and I mean for good—out of our lives. No visits, no calls. Christmases and birthdays came and went without a gift or even a card. And it was all Mama's fault, I was convinced. *She* cut him, *she* called the cops, *she* ran him away—that's all I was able to see. When I found out she had divorced him, I hated Mama for throwing Daddy away. Then, years later, I hated her for remarrying, ironically to a man with my father's real name: Charles, Charles Coleman, an insurance salesman.

I made up my mind from the get-go that Charles would never be a father to me. My father would one day come back, or at least come get me, I daydreamed. Whenever we were in the car going shopping or running some other errand, I was always on the lookout, hoping to catch sight of my father. And one day my dream came true.

We were in the beige Olds. Stepfather Charles and Mama had picked me up from school. Bonnie and Mark were in the car, too, when for the first time in about five years—I saw him.

"Daddy!" I yelled out the window.

My father looked our way, spotted us, took off.

Bonnie, Mark and I—we scrambled from the car and gave chase, but Daddy was in the wind.

My mother understood he was running away from child support. All I saw was Daddy running away from me.

2

COME 2 MY HOUSE

So I was pretty much raised by a tight little tribe of women. We weren't always happy but we were always one big family.

There was tall, regal, but *superstrict* Aunt Barbara who loved her sister's children, but thought we were spoiled.

There was Gramma Maude's older sister, chain-smoking Anna Mae, who taught Bonnie and me to hit it at Tunk and Rummy 500. And that woman sure cussed wicked.

Great-Aunt Anna Mae also had a passion for playing the ponies. Sometimes when I'm performing, the euphoria I experience is akin to the charge I felt when I was with Great-Aunt Anna Mae at the racetrack: that huge, heady moment when the horses hit the finish, and the whole crowd is in unison, one mighty rush of emotions.

Great-Aunt Anna Mae also loved the blues, which made no sense to me because the blues always made me feel lousy. More than the blues, Great-Aunt Anna Mae loved babies, perhaps because she couldn't have children. After her divorce, she became something of a nomad, moving in with whoever needed her. When a cousin, Aunt Barbara, or my mother had a baby, Anna Mae was glad to help out, and she was always happy to babysit later on down the road.

Whenever she babysat us, Bonnie and I had free reign to cuss, something Mama definitely did not approve of. Neither did Gramma Maude's mother, Sallie Johnson, a devout Baptist, and not much of a talker. Great-Gramma Sallie was a permanent fixture in my young life, but the most I remember about interacting with her was when she sent Bonnie and me to the mart to buy her snuff.

Only eight years older than me, Aunt Kathy, from Gramma Maude's brief second marriage, was more big sister than aunt. Gramma Maude made Bonnie and me Kathy's birth control whenever we spent time at their house on Vernon. Wherever Kathy went, Bonnie and I had to go, whether up the street to the Tastee-Freez, to girl talk on a friend's porch, at the skating rink or to a park. The hot tamales from Mr. Harrison's neighborhood restaurant were so delicious, I realize all these years later, because they were a treat from Kathy. And Kathy loved music as much as I did. Her favorites became mine. Mary Well's "You Beat Me to the Punch" was one.

And of course, there was Gramma Maude, who bowled in a league, played bridge, and went to bed early.

"Who's this pretty lady?" I one day asked Gramma Maude, as I held the *Lady in Satin* album cover in my hands.

"That's Billie Holiday."

Gramma Maude always had music on. Her taste ranged from symphony and opera music (a holdover from her Catholic boarding school days) to dead Elmer's collection of folks like Fats Domino, Sarah Vaughan, Billy Eckstine, Billie Holiday.

I could read. But who was she beyond her name? That's what I was asking.

"This was the last album she made, I think," Gramma Maude went on to say. "She recorded part of it on crutches."

Gramma Maude didn't give me details on Billie's blues. So I let my imagination run amok about the life of this pretty lady with the pony tail and bare shoulders, singing in pain.

I felt so sorry for her, singing those songs Gramma Maude enjoyed—"I'm a Fool to Want You". . . "You Don't Know What Love Is". . . "You've Changed". . . "The End of a Love Affair." I heard so many things in her voice. Vulnerability, sadness, a strain of the tragic, are among the things I heard, but couldn't articulate back then. And I truly felt her calling to me. Years later, when I started making music, I forgot all about her—for a while, anyway.

Most of my mother's clan lived together. About two years after my father left, we moved out of Hyde Park and into a brick house Gramma Maude and Aunt Barbara had purchased on 78th and Carpenter, block busting an Irish neighborhood.

My mother, Bonnie, Mark and I lived on the first floor, with my half Lab/half Doberman, Mimi. Gramma Maude, Great-Gramma Sallie, and Aunt Kathy lived on the second floor. Superstrict Aunt Barbara, an elementary school teacher, lived over in Lake Meadows, where she taught ballet lessons on Saturdays—classes she tried at one point to get Bonnie and me to take seriously. We went a few times, and we liked dance well enough, but in our minds, Aunt Barbara was too much of a stickler. She was really into things like us showing up regularly, showing up on time. All that jazz seemed really ridiculous to Bonnie and me. Ditto on Aunt Barbara's diet talk around the time I was graduating from elementary school. She had a problem with my being chubby.

"I like the way I am," I told her. And so what if I was still sucking my thumb!

The member of the family who most fascinated me lived Northside, in a senior citizens complex: Great-Gramma Naomi Bagby, Mama's seven-times-married paternal grandmother, who was a Kansas City bootlegger and quasi-madam turned spiritualist in Chicago.

When I was a child, my mother told me stories about what Gramma Bagby was like when she was in her prime: how she held revivals once a year on South Park, ministering to people in an outfit she concocted that was similar to a nun's habit. Healing was the core of her ministry.

At one point, Great-Gramma Bagby held small services in her one-bedroom apartment above a tavern on State Street (where State Street projects now stand). Along with prayer,

"Mother Bagby," as her followers called her, dispensed oils and candles she had blessed. But Great-Gramma Bagby wasn't all heavenly-minded; she sometimes sidelined in the numbers racket.

The artifacts of Great-Gramma Bagby's life, which Aunt Barbara preserved, blow my mind. There's a program for a sixth annual "Mystery-Prayer-Testimonial and Healing Service." The date: Sunday October 27, '46, 3 to 6 P.M. The place: The Naomi Temple No. 1, Inc., at 4941 South Parkway.

There's Great-Gramma Bagby's diploma, dated September 19, '43, from the Mme. Ryder Barnes School of Metaphysics, where she successfully made her way through the course on "Forty Mystic Degrees and Science of Soul Power."

Aunt Barbara also held onto the horseshoe Great-Gramma Bagby nailed above her bedroom door, and a few of her books, with her musings and eurekas scribbled in the margins: *In Tune with the Infinite* by one of the papas of the New Thought movement, Ralph Waldo Trine; *Metaphysics and the Art of Attainment* by James Payne; and the Unity textbook, *Lessons in Truth* by the homeopath H. Emilie Cady. Great-Gramma Bagby had requested that her body be donated to science.

Mama always said there was a lot of Naomi Bagby in me. And there's truth to that. Great-Gramma Bagby ate in ways others found weird. Like spicy scrambled eggs with string beans on the side and oatmeal you had to slice. As a child, I loved scrambled eggs with jelly and hot sauce, and a cheese-and-raisin mix. Today, I get a lot of "How can you eat that?" about some of my culinary creations.

Great-Gramma Bagby was short. I'm short. But the true tie that binds is the healing. I've always seen myself as a healer, with my songs, with my singing. Of course, I'm not claiming to have healed diseases, but so many people have told me that my song has made them feel better. And I feel that, too.

In the mid-1970s, after dementia set in, Great-Gramma Bagby spent her last days with Aunt Barbara, by then living in a house in Hyde Park. One day Great-Gramma Bagby fell down some steps, was taken to the hospital and never returned.

I was on the road when Great-Gramma Bagby passed. To this day I can get a bit prickly when I remember how I found out—after the fact—after the memorial service—after I got back to Chicago. My family thought they were sparing me. They feared I'd freak out if I got the news long distance.

Great-Gramma Bagby's complexities and contradictions still intrigue me and inspire me to reconstruct her life for deeper insight into mine. Think about it, here was this black woman in the '40s being a leader, making her life on her terms, and craving to transcend, not be earth-bound. There sure *is* a lot of Naomi Bagby in me.

My strongest memory of her is the time she read my palm.

"One day many, many people will know your name . . ."

I was six or seven.

". . . for something you do with your hands."

Great-Gramma Bagby delivered no specifics. But because she looked and sounded so wise, I had no doubts that she knew what she was talking about.

3

DESTINY

Art? I wondered some days, because that's certainly something people do with their hands and I loved to draw, to paint. The sculpture set my parents had bought me was one of the best gifts ever—second only perhaps to the dollhouse they made for Bonnie and me: our Christmas present one year when they didn't have money for fabulous store-bought gifts. That was the best Christmas ever. Given my parents' love of art, it's not surprising that I sometimes wanted to be an artist. When it came to school days, my favorite part was the after-school arts-and-crafts program I was in for a time.

The other part of my school days—first at Kozminski, then at Saint Sabina, where I was the only black girl in my class—were fairly uneventful and boring, except for the public school bullies.

"*Chinks!*" they taunted Bonnie and me. Even more than today, our eyes had that "Asiany," thing going on when we were young. We never took any great pride in our eyes, never thought them a good thing or bad thing—they just were. Our eyes mattered a whole lot more to the bullies than to us. They also had a problem with our clothes.

Bonnie and I were often dressed like twins, and so they picked on us for "trying to be cute." We had better clothes—always the latest styles—than them. They thought we were something like rich. But we knew better.

I once tried to tell the bullies our mother couldn't afford a lot of store-bought stuff. I told them that she made most of our clothes. That only made matters worse. Can Mama make them some clothes they wanted to know. They wanted me to take home orders. They didn't want to hear that Mama didn't have time to make everybody's clothes. So then, it was like I was being selfish, stuck-up. But I wasn't! I wasn't! I wasn't! In truth, I was a sharer. I remember the time a friend was over our place, and she oohed-and-aahed over a fruit basket on our kitchen table.

"You can have it," I said.

I was always giving stuff away. My stuff, Mama's stuff. I didn't care if it got me in trouble. If I felt something would make somebody happy—"You can have it."

When I told Mama about the bullies, "Take them one at a time," she advised. I was ready to do that the day a pack of five or six crowded around Bonnie and me.

But the pack wasn't going for any one-at-a-time. They jumped us. Bonnie and I fought back as best we could (Bonnie was always the better fighter). At one point, when I got my ankle caught in the bottom of a chain-link fence and saw blood, we just ran, ran, ran—making it home, by sheer luck, without too much damage done. Today, all I have to do is glance or finger that scar on my ankle and I'm back in that moment, the moment I decided I was tired of getting my butt kicked, and was going to get me some advantage.

The next day, I took the little knife from my sculpture set to school. If anybody messed with me, I was going to use it. As it turned out, the only thing that happened that day was that a teacher somehow got wind of my "weapon" and I got suspended. (But at least I didn't get jumped.)

When it came to class time, my mind wandered a lot. At times, I felt as if was doing stuff I'd already done. Only the science classes tended to grab me. Because I liked animals, some days I thought maybe I'd become a vet. When I learned the words *anthropology* and *archaeology,* some days I daydreamed of getting into those fields. I don't remember what it was I read or saw on TV that made me think going on digs in Egypt would be great! Other days I thought about becoming a nun.

I wasn't really raised Catholic, but like everyone else who attended Saint Sabina, I also had to attend its church next door. It was as huge and magnificent to a child's eyes as Notre Dame. The feeling of vastness I experienced in that church, the incense, the holy, heaven-bound music—it all romanced my soul, made me want to be devout, close to God. And nuns definitely seemed that—as well as powerful, and givers of things good and bad. Plus, I dug the Franciscan nuns' habit.

But I'd never heard of a famous nun. *Does smacking a kid count as something you do with your hands?* I wondered one day, both remembering Great-Gramma Bagby's prophecy and that creaky, old nun who slapped me. I can't remember why— only that her slap didn't much sting. She was slow, not in sync. I felt more wind than hand.

I began to back off the nun thing, after what happened during catechism one day. I asked the priest something to the effect of "Are you saying that to believe in God we have to trust in Him without question?"

It seemed to me that they were telling us not to use our minds, whereas I understood—and I believed—that it was God who had created us, had given us fantastic minds. If we were God's children, how could He be happy if we didn't use all the gifts He gave us?

The priest was not pleased. He sent me to Mother Superior, who gave me something of a tongue-lashing, tried to scare me out of questioning things. After that, my feelings about nuns and becoming one went limp.

Singing? Never. I never even daydreamed of growing up to be a professional singer. Singing was just something Bonnie and I did for fun. We were always singing around the house, singing for family, singing for Mama's friends at her card parties.

It was for the sheer love of singing, that when I was around eleven, Bonnie and I formed a group with two friends from school, Finesse and Nikki. When it came to the name of our group, the weather was the inspiration.

Mama had let us sit out on the stoop. First snow was falling, softening the night, and it was going to be a doozie. We were trying to find a name for our group as we watched wonders in the making—the twinkling of flakes in the streetlights, icy snow dusting the streets. Of course, we suddenly thought about "The Snowflakes." Not sparkly enough.

"How 'bout 'The Crystals'?" I said. Then, since the suffix "ette" was all the rage for girl-groups back, we settled on "The Crystalettes."

The Crystalettes entered talent shows at youth centers, clubs, and other venues. Our chief competition was a group of sisters who had shifted from gospel to pop. Originally, they'd been known as the Heavenly Sunbeams, then as the Hutchinson Sunbeams, and later as The Emotions (yes, of "Best of My Love" fame).

The Crystalettes won a lot. Sometimes there was an actual prize (maybe fifty bucks). Other times, the winner was the group with the most money thrown at them on the stage.

The Crystalettes not only sounded good, we looked good, too. Thanks to Mama. Along with making time to chaperone us, she made time to make us beautiful outfits, such as fruity colored A-line dresses with mandarin collars. We felt so grown up after she did our makeup. (Obviously, I wasn't hating Mama at those moments.) She really went above and beyond in support of our fun. She had even gotten us a piano and piano lessons—which, unfortunately, quickly went the way of Aunt Barbara's dance classes.

Like most every other teen group, The Crystalettes covered a lot of top 40 tunes: Gladys Knight and the Pips' "Grapevine," Dionne Warwick's "Message to Michael," and the Queen of Soul's "Chain of Fools" and "R-E-S-P-E-C-T."

Yeah, I got a little kick out of being called "Little Aretha," but I never wanted *to be* Aretha. Singing was just a natural thing to do. I thought everybody sang and played music during Saturday morning chores. To me singing was like breathing, or peeing—just a normal, necessary function. What with my father's love of music, and that of Gramma Maude, Great-Aunt Anna Mae, Aunt Kathy—plus, my mother had a thing for *Madame Butterfly;* she was crazy about Nina Simone; and the vocal style and range of the Peruvian singer-actress Yma Sumac knocked her out. So, I can truly say I lived in music. And as they say, it's hardly the fish that discovers the water.

All the love and genius (and quirks) I absorbed from the womenfolk in my world notwithstanding, I sometimes envied friends who were growing up with fathers in the house—fathers who called them "Princess" maybe. When you've never known your father, there's a hole, a missing. But when you have known your father, when you've been a daddy's girl, the void and longing, I think, is even worse. Had he died I probably would have handled it better than his just being *gone,* somewhere out there away from me. Then again, for all I knew he could have been dead.

I not only "lost" my father at ten, I also didn't have what

other friends had, surrogate fathers—granddads and lots of uncles to tell them stories and buy them things their parents wouldn't, and other male relatives who could give you a clue as to what you should look for in a boyfriend or husband when you grow up. Uncle Roy and I were close, but when he and Aunt Barbara divorced—*Poof!* He was out of my life. As for my father's father, I recall only seeing him once or twice (and speaking to Grandmother Marie perhaps a couple of times on the phone).

When my mother started dating Charles Coleman, Bonnie, Mark, and I were happy for her because he seemed to make her happy. When I found out they were going to marry, I wasn't sure what that would mean for my life (though I did vow that he would *never* be a father to me). Thankfully, the marriage didn't result in our leaving our neighborhood. We only moved around the corner, into a house on Morgan, the first home my sister Tammy knew.

The day Tammy was born, July 19, '68—what a jubilee, one of the brightest days of my youth. Ever since I was little, I had loved babies. When Mark and I played "commercials," our game sometimes wandered into what kind of life we'd have when we grew up. One thing I knew for sure, I was going to have some babies! I even decided on the names I'd give them—can't for the life of me remember them now—but anyway, I couldn't wait to be grown: I'd have babies, babies, babies! Of course, when I got grown I found out that loving babies is one thing—and easy—whereas raising children is a whole other matter.

But back in the summer of '68 I thought taking care of babies would be nothing but fun. And my mother let me name my new sister.

My mother had wanted another boy so badly. She was so super certain the baby would be a boy, she hadn't even brainstormed on girls' names. When she saw her beautiful little baby girl she was stumped—couldn't come up with a name good enough for her.

"Name her 'Tammy,'" I said. *Tammy and the Bachelor; Tammy Tell Me True; Tammy and the Doctor; Tammy and the Millionaire,* Tammy of the "cottonwoods whisperin" and the "hooty-owls hoot-hooing to the doves"—thanks to Debbie Reynolds and then Sandra Dee, a lot of us had the name "Tammy" on the brain.

I was always able to separate Tammy from her father, loving her to death, even while I gave Charles Coleman hell: sassing back, igging him, defying anything close to an order, griping about him to my mother. No way in the world did I want *him* to call me Princess.

I remember once getting him so riled he crashed his fist through a wall.

"He tried to kill me!" I was in tears when I told my mother all about it over the phone. (He had not even been aiming for me.)

When my mother and Charles divorced, I was like "Good riddance!" yet all the while I felt a little guilty. I knew they had had their "issues," stuff that had nothing to do with me. But I also knew I'd spiced the strife to a certain degree. Am I ever glad he didn't die when I was still in my teens, and that the day would come when I'd apologize and we'd be something like family.

4

S O   N A U G H T Y

"You're *drunk!*"

I was definitely no longer thinking about becoming a nun. Being free, doing as I pleased was uppermost on my mind. I played hooky a lot. I hung out with kids my mother called "bad company."

I had toughened up a lot, too. Not only had I honed my fighting skills, I also knew how to prep for optimum advantage.

Oh, you wanna fight me? All I needed was a quick minute to take off my earrings and grease my face and I was ready to rumble!

Bonnie and I had our share of showdowns, going at each other as hard as we did against challengers in the street. Punching, scratching at each others' faces, grabbing hair—

hoping to yank some out—throwing each other's clothes straight out the window. Over what? Maybe I'd used something of hers without asking, or vice versa. Maybe one of us snapped on the other when the other wasn't in a joking mood.

Yep, we had hit the terrible teens. It comes as no surprise to anyone who has raised children that our mother got the brunt of our madness. I was back to blaming her for my father's absence, back to believing, as I had when I was much younger, that I sometimes got slapped, not for something I'd done, but simply because I looked like my father.

Bonnie and I blew our mother's fuse I don't know how many times. Inch by inch I was fighting for ground, struggling to break free from her cage of expectations. I was working hard at not being scared of her, too.

"MC" my friends called her. When "Mother Coleman," passed them on the street—with her thanks-to-ballet ramrod straight back, horn-rim glasses, head up, serious-business face, pocketbook clutched tight—they gave her a wide birth and respect. Not me.

One evening when I was AWOL—hadn't come home from school, hadn't done my chores—MC went looking for me. When she found me, she embarrassed the hell out of me—giving me a pretty good ass-whipping right there in the street! in my own neighborhood!

I guess she thought I'd learned a lesson. But I kept going AWOL, staggering in one night, a bit past midnight.

"I'm not drunk!" I shot back. When Mama started in with her fussing, I lost my mind, and for the first time in my life, I wasn't just giving her lip, I was cussing her out.

Next thing I knew, she had me up against a wall by my neck. My feet touched air.

When I broke loose—*This is it! This is it. This is the time!* I had known this day was coming. My mother and I could not— would *never!*—get along, I was sure. She had Mark and Tammy to still baby. Didn't she get it that I was no longer a child? Fuck MC and her rules and demands.

"If you're not coming straight home after school, at least let me know where you'll be?"

Sometimes I don't know where I'll be until I get there.

"Clean up your room!"

If the mess doesn't bother me why should it bother you?

"Stop sneaking your friends into the house after I've gone to sleep!"

Dang.

I was not going to be *oh-pressed!*

If my mother thought slamming me up against a wall would teach me a lesson, she had another thing coming; I had other plans.

I ran away from home (and not for the first time) with nothing else but Mimi. We landed in Hyde Park, in a place where I figured I could be free.

5

STREET PLAYER

I had my sources. After walking around for a while, I tucked into a phone booth and called a cousin I thought might know where my father was. As it turned out, she had a phone number, and a shocker for me: Daddy had remarried, to some white chick.

White Chick was the one who answered the phone. Since my father wasn't there, I went ahead and told her my "plight."

"Come on over," she said. She gave me the address. It was on Ingleside, not very far from where we had once lived.

Mimi and I walked way across town to 54th and Ingleside, to a limestone townhouse. Constance Faye Stevens welcomed me to call her Connie. She was a schoolteacher I later discovered, and one unlike any other I'd ever known. Connie was a free-spirit like I wanted to be, a woman who thought nothing of going about braless and who was rumored to sometimes garden topless.

People have asked if I freaked out about my father taking up with a white woman. Not at all. Had she been really bossy or snotty to me, hell yeah, then I would have freaked out. But because she was cool, I was cool with her.

I also discovered that my father never stopped loving his children, that he'd missed me. He had stayed away, thinking Mama would be vindictive. I was more than willing to accept this. I wasn't in a frame of mind to press him, perhaps because I didn't want to press myself and come to the conclusion that fear of Mama was a flimsy excuse for doing the bird—physically, emotionally, financially—on your children. I was with my father again. That's all that mattered to me then.

My mother had her sources, too. After going half out of her mind, calling everyone, anyone, she could think of—*Have you seen Yvette?*—she got a call from one of my father's neighbors to let her know I was okay.

After a couple of days with my father and Connie, I was back with MC. But I didn't want to stay. Bonnie—ditto. We begged her to let us live with our father, and, finally, she consented. Even Mark later joined us for a time.

I gave no thought to how hurtful it might be to have your children beg to leave you. After all my mother had done to keep us fed, clothed, sheltered, going the extra mile for my Crystalette desires—like many teens, I was perfectly self-absorbed, an absolute ingrate. Did it occur to me that it might gall her that after all she had done for me, I wanted nothing more than to be with the man who hadn't done jack for me in years? Hell, no.

By the time I began getting to know my father again, he had reinvented himself. A couple of times. Soon after he left us, he moved to New York, living in Greenwich Village for a time. At one point, he was a shipping clerk for a newspaper company. At another point, he was building sets for off-Broadway theater companies. He had returned to Chicago in '66, the year he married Connie. And he ended up becoming a photographer.

Daddy took a course at the Illinois Institute of Technology and then he took it from there. He went on to teach photography (and drama) at the same school where Connie taught. He also freelanced for book publishers (working mostly on children's books). He made hundreds of portraits of children. Daddy had put on his travelin' shoes, too. His photographs from places he visited sparked my desire to see the world.

"I must see this!" I thought as he showed me photos from his trip to Ibiza. When he told me that in Spain children drank wine like we drank pop—well, you can imagine the visions that danced through my head.

Living with my father and Connie—I was loving it! loving it! I was free to take in all the cool cultural stuff going on in the Hyde Park area—lots of good jazz, cafes, open air concerts, beatniks and hippies hanging out. My father and Connie didn't care if Bonnie and I smoked weed because they smoked weed, too.

My father, as mad about Dostoevsky as he was about jazz, was such a reader! such a philosopher! I felt I was learning more from him than I could ever learn in a million years of school. He hepped me to EST and nuggets of Nietzsche. Music was almost always on during our discussions—from Miles, Ella, and Joni Mitchell to the Beatles.

My father was playing *Abbey Road* for me the first time I dropped acid. He had told me that if I ever wanted to try a drug I should let him know because he could probably get it for me. If I was going to experiment, he figured it would be better if he were with me so he could monitor the situation. He didn't want me tripping around a bunch of strangers or friends who might only panic if I freaked out. There was a certain logic to that. But I know there were (and are) people who wanted to whip him, make him Exhibit A for bad parenting.

But you have to remember the times. America was in a cultural revolution, with clarion calls for change, change, change in every area of life, including parenting: Let your children call you by your first name! Be friends with your kids! Get high with your kids!

I'm not saying people should blame their behavior on the "times," only that some people go with the flow of the Zeitgeist, and some people don't. My father did. Plus, what did he know about parenting? He had had practically none in his childhood.

His mother had been so vain that she continued wearing a girdle while pregnant with him (maybe that's why he was a low-birth-weight baby). Plus, she was a floozy. Grandfather Charles was a Pullman Porter, so when the cat was away . . . Although, to be fair, my grandmother didn't start stepping out on my grandfather until telltale signs of other women started turning up in his traveling bag.

Charles, Sr.'s times on the road (often two weeks at a clip), became Marie's times to take off. This left my father and his older sister to take care of their four younger sibs, and grateful for the times when their paternal grandmother, "Big Mama," came by with a bag of groceries.

You'd think after being abandoned by his own mother, my father would have thought twice about running out on us. Then again, you'd think I would have done everything I could to avoid my kids ever feeling abandoned. So maybe the lesson is, unless you're really careful history will repeat itself; we are much more comfortable doing what we know rather than doing what we know is right.

My father had to do a lot of hustling to survive. He shined shoes in a barbershop, built fences, fancied up people's yards with shrubs scavenged from around the railroad tracks behind Montgomery Ward. For a time, he was helper to a man who sold fruits and vegetables from a horse-drawn cart. Sometimes, he and his little gang swiped cartons of sweets off trucks at the loading docks of Hershey's and other Northside candy factories. Usually, my father was the gang's salesman, and he had no problem unloading the candy because there were beaucoup folks who had no compunction about buying boosted goods.

With his share of the "earnings," my father usually bought

stuff like chili and pop. And songbooks. He always had one of those in his back pocket, even when tennis shoes were his only winter footwear.

After his parents split up, my father had even less "quality" *or* "quantity" time with his father. But he did get to see him before he entered the service. For a last hurrah, his father took him and a friend who was Army-bound to the grand Chicago Theater for dinner and Nat King Cole—live! For my father, that was like a million bucks. He and his father had had a recent falling out, and hadn't been speaking, so this boys' night out was a fare-thee-well and a make-up rolled up in one.

My father did not tell me the story of his childhood in one fell swoop, but over time. The more I learned about what a jagged upbringing he had, the more I sorry I felt for him, the more I understood that, when it came to being a father, maybe he had done the best he could. I certainly understood why he may have thought my mother's dancing was a smoke screen for infidelity.

After *Abbey Road,* my father turned me on to a little Bob Dylan. We were sipping beer as we listened, and having a hell of a deep conversation, the substance of which I wish I could remember with half the clarity I remember buying my first album (Led Zeppelin), being heavy into Hendrix, and thinking school was total BS.

Living with Daddy meant transferring to another high school,

Kenwood Academy. When I went, I was mostly into rapping with other cool kids—some black, some white, some other—about how messed up the world was, about the revolution we needed. Sometimes we sipped our white port and Kool-Aid mix, most of us sporting combat boots, and rapped about the plight of the Black Nation.

Lots of rapping—we had opinions on everything. We rapped about what black people needed to do: learn their true history, stop taking crap from white folks, et cetera et cetera.

We rapped about what white people needed to do: learn *their* true history, get their feet off black folks' necks, et cetera et cetera. The world would truly be a better place, I believed, if more whites were like Connie, who didn't cringe when I put up posters of Mark Clark and Fred Hampton. Connie understood what the Black Panther Party was, at root, and what they were trying to achieve. She didn't buy the propaganda that they were just a bunch of wild-dog thugs. Connie was cooler, more hep, than a lot of kids at Kenwood.

And heaven forbid one of the Kenwood squares came up to me with something like, "So, are you going to the Sock Hop tonight?" because I had an opinion about that, too.

"No, I'm not going to the Sock Hop tonight! That's *slave* shit."

Homework? That was "slave shit," too, I thought, because as far as I could see they weren't teaching us anything R-E-L-E-VANT! (I just *knew* I had the world figured out.)

And I had only one word for anybody who was not down with our program—*stupidmuthafucker!*

45

Along with all that "slave shit," I was shedding all the old, dead, dull language. I was no Negro—I was Black! I was a chick who dug the far-out, the outta-sight, the groovy, the people who planned love-ins, and went psychedelic, refashioning their lives with gypsy and paisley patterns, fringe and beads, and buttons—Turn On, Tune In, Drop Out; Ban the Bra; Hands Off Tim Leary; Suppose They Gave a War and Nobody Came?; Power to the People.

I instigated protests and mini-riots—for black studies, the ouster of the principal, the school admin to otherwise get it together—just as I had done as head of Calumet High's Afro-American Student Organization—CASO. At Calumet, I had gotten arrested a few times for setting off cherry bombs in the lunchroom, organizing walk-outs; fighting off *stupidmuthafucking* cops!

LeRoi Jones-turned-Amiri Baraka penned my SOS:

Calling black people
Calling all black people, man woman child
Wherever you are, calling you, urgent, come in
Black People, come in, wherever you are, urgent, calling
you, calling all black people
calling all black people, come in, black people, come
on in.

Bonnie and I tried writing poetry like Baraka's. I had a jones for The Last Poets, too. Not that I needed to look to Newark or Harlem for inspiration and great griots. Chicago was home to that absolute truth-teller Gwendolyn Brooks. And there was Don L. Lee (later Haki Madhubuti), and Brooks's other protégés, some of whom were in on the creation of the Organization of Black American Culture, aka OBAC.

I got fired up by Cleaver's *Soul on Ice,* Greenlee's *Spook,* and *Go Tell It on the Mountain, The Fire Next Time*—just about everything Baldwin wrote. I was broadening my horizons when it came to music, too, finding my way into Yusef Lateef and Bird, for starters. I felt so free! So alive! So aware!

Bonnie and I had started becoming more aware of our African heritage at an old movie house transformed into a cultural center, on 39th and Pershing, the Affro-Arts Theater.

The concept was something of an outgrowth of the truly visionary Association for the Advancement of Creative Musicians. AACM's mission: to advance free jazz and liberate artists from the claws of commercialism. Their Motto: "Great Black Music: Ancient to the Future."

Affro-Arts was the brainchild of an AACM cofounder, multi-instrumentalist and musicologist Phil Cohran, a member of Sun-Ra's Arkestra until Sun-Ra quit Chicago and kicked it to New York. Eventually, Affro-Arts was run by a group once known as the Artistic Heritage Ensemble: The Pharaohs, alma pater of some of the guys who birthed Earth, Wind, and Fire.

Sadly, the Affro-Arts space ended up becoming a hangout for the notorious Blackstone Rangers, got raided, and was eventually torn down. Looking through an Affro-Arts brochure Aunt Barbara managed to hang onto for more than thirty years, brought it all back. How vibrant, how dynamic, how beautiful

Affro-Arts was! And BOLD!—billing itself as "the only contin-
uous valid black experience in the midwestern sector of the
United States." This, at a time when wearing African garb
wasn't a mere whim or fashion statement and you didn't have
corporations making the mad dash to turn "Afrocentric" into
just another commodity or marketing shtick.

Affro-Arts offered us art exhibits, dance classes, lectures, poetry readings by Brooks and OBAC, and performances by
Roland Kirk, Olatunji, and the Ghana Dance Ensemble. There
were showings of all sorts of films, from Baraka's *Dutchman* to
Africa Addio. And concerts by the Pharaohs, of course.

Some thirty years later, as I looked at the brochure's group
photo of the Pharaohs, I struggled to put names to faces. Thank
goodness for the captions!—"Pharaoh Nora, Pharaoh Aaron,
Pharaoh Willie, Pharaoh Don, Pharaoh Beni, Pharaoh Bob,"
Pharaoh on and on.

On other pages of the brochure, I found collages of photos
from Affro-Arts events—many of those peoples' names were on
the tip of my tongue! Their photos were used above captions to
illustrate that, as the organization put it, "The Affro-Arts Theater is . . . Black dance . . . Black Music . . . and Black harmony.
It is Black Students . . . And Black Poets . . . And Talented Black
Families . . . and Lovely Black Sisters!!"

Above that last caption, a photo of four girls, all of us with
afros, and me with one hand on a hip, looking, I suppose, as
I'm-black-and-I'm-proud as I could. We flank a huge painting
of Malcolm X.

At Affro-Arts, Bonnie and I learned to make our own geles

and dashikis. We went veggie, baked our own bread. We were usually in the weekly variety show.

Bonnie and I had morphed our group into The Shades of Black. With two new girls, Zuri and Mokeya, we often sang songs from the Motherland, modeling Makeba. I was doing it all phonetically; I had no idea what I was singing. But we sounded good. And sometimes my father was there, taking photograph after photograph of The Shades of Black. He was making up for all the snapshots he'd missed out on due to his hasty exit.

With The Shades of Black, I got my first taste of touring: a time or two with The Emotions, The Staple Singers, and once with Mary Wells, or so I'm told. To be honest, I really don't remember that.

This taste of touring happened when we were still living with our mother, so we didn't get to go on as many trips as we would have liked. If she was unable to chaperone or find someone else she trusted to do so, the answer was always "Absolutely not!"

Great-Aunt Anna Mae was our chaperone the time we went to D.C. with the Pharaohs, Bobby "Get-Down" Brown, and Darlene Blackburn's fabulous Afro-Cuban dance troupe. We performed at an outdoor festival on The Hill. Performing was only part of the thrill. There was a lot of cutting up and laughter on the bus, a lot of giggling and whispering in our hotel room at night, and more than one girl lost their virginity during that trip. But not me. Sure, I liked boys, but I was not in a hurry for sex. At least not yet. And no, I *still* had no dreams of becoming a professional singer.

"Are you having sex?" Connie asked because she knew about my very first boyfriend, Rahman, a onetime gangbanger who changed his ways and become a Dashiki-wearing down-with-the-movement brother, part of the Affro-Arts community.

I lied. "Yes." I guess I felt going *almost* all the way counted.

Connie took me to get birth control pills. Only they didn't work for me; they made me sick. And anyway, birth control became irrelevant because it was evidently not meant for me and Rahman to go all the way. But I will forever cherish the good times I had with him and his brother "Sugarbear." Just as I will forever cherish my Affro-Arts days, which were so important in me becoming me—and coming into a new name.

Once a year a Yoruba priest came to Affro-Arts to hold a naming ceremony, choosing names based on people's orishas, or guiding spirits.

The Baba proclaimed me:

Chaka—"Woman of Fire,"
Adunne—"Loves to Touch,"
Aduffe—"Someone Others Love to Touch,"
Yemoja—"Mother of the Waters,"
Hodarhi—"Woman of Nature,"
Karifi—"Strength."

A lot to live up to, maybe, but everything seemed possible back then. It was the dawning of the Age of Aquarius and a man had walked on the moon.

Had I not been so impatient to have an African name I would have had Igbo ones, instead of Yoruba, because that's what Aunt Barbara's second husband, Ben, a former soccer star in Nigeria, was. Uncle Ben was going to give Bonnie and me names, but to my mind he took too long to think it through. Bonnie jumped the gun, too, and went Yoruba as well, besting me by one name: Taka Hodarhi Osune Adenidi Asake Bobtito Ayoka.

How do I feel about my Yoruba names all these years later? Cool. They suit me (though I don't know about the "mother of the waters"). And as I said in an interview, there are times I wish one of my names had been a word that translated into something like "She who takes no shit." If names are destiny or at least shape personality, with a name like that—I might have handled a lot of things differently. But then again, maybe not.

6

DEMOCRAZY

During the fall of '69, I was hanging out a lot at Loop City College, later renamed Harold Washington, for Chicago's first black mayor.

I wasn't auditing classes at Loop. I was there because that's where the Panthers held a lot of meetings: planning sessions for walkouts, boycotts, rallies, and assorted other movement work, organized by, among others, the matchless Fred Hampton.

Fred had been evincing some serious leadership skills for years by the time I met him: as head of Maywood's NAACP Youth Council and as founder and chairman of Black Panther Party's Illinois chapter, headquartered on Chicago's Southside.

Setting up food pantries and a health clinic; organizing recreational programs for children and political education classes (for all comers); negotiating truces between gangs; working to transform thugs into heroes—Fred delivered so much more than rhetoric.

I remember wondering if he ever had a good bellylaugh, ever cut up and clowned around. For all I know, perhaps he did in private. But whenever I saw him he was in movement-mode. He was like an army sergeant. Not that I ever saw him be cruel to anyone. He might put a friendly arm around your shoulder by way of encouragement—"Hello, Sister Chaka," but he wasn't about a lot of chit-chat. Fred was all about "the struggle."

And I was so down with the BPP Ten-Point Program back then: "WE WANT freedom. We want power to determine the destiny of our Black Community. WE WANT full employment for our people. . . . WE WANT decent housing, fit for the shelter of human beings. . . . WE WANT education for our people that exposes the true nature of this decadent American society. We want education that teaches us our true history and our role in the present-day society. . . . WE WANT an immediate end to POLICE BRUTALITY and MURDER of black people."

It all sounded so righteous, so strong and right, so *what-the-hell-have-we-got-to-lose!* It was half-past time for us to be BOLD!, I believed.

Those were desperate, angry times. We had lived through years of civil rights movement fatalities, with the slayings of Evers, Malcolm, and King at the top of the litany. By the late '60s, many of us, especially those of us living Up South, had serious doubts that we would overcome the police brutality and all the other nigger treatment via a movement that was meek-and-mild.

Even though I was only two when one of Chicago's native sons was brutalized in Money, Mississippi, I mourned Emmett Till. His murder was one of those "never-forget" incidents. I don't know too many black people of my generation who, as children, weren't told what had happened to Emmett, and who weren't shown that gruesome photo that first appeared in *Jet*. He was a teenager when they did that to him. As a teenager, I wasn't convinced the same shit couldn't happen to me or Bonnie, or one of our friends. And so, there I was selling *The Black Panther* on street corners. I was also heading up a free breakfast program for children in an old Southside church. And one day I was in possession of a gun.

It wasn't a Panther's gun. It belonged to a security guard at Loop, where some BPP comrades and I had gone to watch (for the millionth time) Pontecorvo's *The Battle for Algiers*—getting schooled on another people's fight to throw off colonial rule. It was an "unauthorized" activity in a classroom someone had found empty.

We didn't get to the end of the film because suddenly the lights came on and in strode Mr. Guard, everything coming out of his mouth all wrong, all obnoxious, barking at us to "Get out!"

He got jumped for his troubles. In the ruckus, I ended up with his gun: a .38 long-nosed Colt.

I kept that gun for months, toying with the idea of doing

something radical, daring myself to—*Chaka, this is your chance to step up to bat!* Offing a Pig perhaps? Some random whitey? I even did a little target practice at a rifle range.

I told no one I had the gun, not even Bonnie. But my secret slowly made me sick to my stomach. I wondered if I was getting an ulcer. And was I violating one of the BPP's "3 Main Rules of Discipline"?

TURN IN EVERYTHING CAPTURED FROM THE ATTACKING ENEMY.

Is that security guard the enemy?

I began to wonder what offing a pig would accomplish. I flashed back to summers before, to the days of flames, the riots. Violence, violence, violence, in Newark, Watts, Harlem, Chicago. And there was the chaos and rage in April '68 after word spread that King had been slain. Then, two months later, Bobby Kennedy was shot. Two months after that, the Chicago air was full of tear gas, mingled with screams, crashing glass and burning things, as antiwar warriors and cops went at it during the Democratic National Convention. And in the aftermath, Mayor Daley's Freudian slip: "The policeman isn't there to create disorder, the policeman is there to preserve disorder."

Violence. Nonviolence led to violence. Violence led to violence. I was sick of violence.

All the clenched fists, rallies, speeches, marches, protests—I couldn't say nothing had changed, but I was starting to have my doubts that the BPP approach could maintain. I started to see that "The Power," "The Man" grew strong on our anger, on chaos, on divisions—black/white, men/women, old/young. What could my one gun do against that?

"You can kill a revolutionary, but you cannot kill the revolution" was one of Fred's most famous sayings. By late '69 I was not such a true believer. I realized, too, I wasn't being true to myself. Yeah, a lot of white folks pissed me off, but I wasn't *really* anti-white. I loved Connie. I had white friends while I was with the BPP. The idea that being pro-black equals being anti-white did not compute for me.

I was thinking maybe I just needed to finish high school and figure out what to do with my life. As for the gun, I hurled that sucker into the University of Chicago's Botany Pond. Immediately, I felt free.

Not long after that, on December 4, '69, I got a call from a BPP comrade: Fred Hampton was dead.

Suspecting the Panthers had some big-ass stash of weapons, about a dozen cops descended on Hampton's apartment. When they knocked on the door, Panthers immediately started shooting—or so went the official version of events. I didn't buy it! Nobody I knew bought it, including Aunt Barbara.

She had been decorating her door when she heard the news. Like so many of us, she sped over to 2337 Monroe Street, to stare in absolute horror at a bullet-riddled place cordoned off by yellow crime-scene tape. We stood in the bitter cold, in shock and disbelief. I think I cried most of that day, and kept thinking of the day Fred came to check out my breakfast program with about eight other Panthers, all in uniform—black leather jacket, black beret, black everything. How proud I felt when without spending a whole lot of words, he let me know I had passed inspection.

When Aunt Barbara returned home from staring at the scene of the shooting, she yanked Santa Claus from her front door, removed all the Christmas decorations from inside her home, and decided she would never again merry up her place for the holidays, or send out Christmas cards.

That bleak December, Aunt Barbara was among the hundreds who wrote letters—to the mayor, to the governor, to the newspapers—and who spoke out on local television and radio shows. "Some justice has to be done," she proclaimed, while the authorities stuck to their script, until—eventually—ballistics evidence proved it bogus. "Execution," "Assassination" some called it then, some call it still.

William O'Neal, Fred's bodyguard and chief of security, a car thief turned FBI informant, had provided the cops with the floor plan and slipped Fred a sedative. So Fred was out cold when the cops raided his home a little after 4 A.M., shooting up the place. Twenty-two-year-old Mark Clark dead from a shot to the chest. Twenty-one-year-old Fred, from four shots to the head.

Among the wounded, Fred's wife, eight months pregnant with their son. Some one hundred shots were fired in all. Only one came from a Panther's gun.

I was among the five thousand at the services, with Ralph Abernathy among the mourners, when Jesse Jackson remarked, "When Fred was shot in Chicago, black people in particular, and decent people in general, bled everywhere."

My brother was with me and maybe he shouldn't have been. Mark was just nine and didn't understand. Then again, neither did I.

To this day, I remember looking into the casket, at the sickening sight of Fred's lifeless face.

Outside, speakers blared Diana Ross and the Supremes' big hit of the year, "Someday We'll Be Together." Nothing made sense to me, except that my days as a radical were over. I didn't put it past the cops to do to me what they'd done to Fred. Yeah, I was shaken up to put it mildly. I was also thinking I wasn't ready to die.

I was going to try hard to get out of high school and figure out how to get into the Art Institute. In the meantime, I threw myself into the one thing I knew I could do that would earn me a little change.

7

DANCE WIT ME

To say that I grew up fast is an understatement. Actually, I didn't really get to grow up—I shot up. In my hurry to freedom, I skipped a lot of steps. I never got to marinate. By age seventeen, you couldn't tell me I wasn't a woman. And woman power was definitely in the air.

Feminism's "Second Wave" was in motion, with black women working what Alice Walker would later term "womanism." It was in '70 that *Essence* first hit the newsstands. What a boost that was for black women, a slick snappy magazine *for us*—where we could learn about ourselves making it in business, medicine, politics, the arts. Not to mention see ourselves being Mod.

For a young black woman, '70 was like a bonanza year. Not

only did we get *Essence,* we got Toni Morrison's *The Bluest Eye* and Toni Cade's manifesto of an anthology, *The Black Woman,* where the sister declared:

> We are involved in a struggle for liberation: liberation
> from the exploitive and dehumanizing system of racism,
> from the manipulative control of a corporate society; lib-
> eration from the constrictive norms of "mainstream" cul-
> ture, from the synthetic myths that encourage us to
> fashion ourselves rashly from without (reaction) rather
> than from within (creation).

Amen to that. She said what I was feeling back then, though I didn't read her book. But another book that came out that year that I did read was Maya Angelou's *I Know Why the Caged Bird Sings.* That was the first book by a black woman I ever read, and I remember loving it. I remember it making me feel spiritually lighter and heavier all at the same time. I could definitely get with the metaphor. I didn't process my feelings back then, but looking back, I now know what it did for me: held out hope while it told truth. Tough, rough, heavy times will be, but so too the overcoming. *Caged Bird* would stay with me over the years, and I still think it beautiful. It was an anchor for the soul during days when *still* all around there was so much chaos, destruction, killing, killing, killing! (Though I now see that that seems to always be the way of humankind.)

Just about every day we were getting hit with some seriously negative shit. U.S. troops in Cambodia! The truth about the My

Lai massacre! The hazard of Agent Orange! National Guardsmen killed four at Kent State! Construction workers on Wall Street went berserk on peaceniks! When I heard about police shooting into a crowd of student protestors—killing two—at Jackson State, I thought, yeah, Nina Simone, "Mississippi Goddam" is right. The spirit of violence was everywhere. Even some anti-war warriors were going wider on the warpath.

The Weathermen, who had rocked Chicago's world with their four "Days of Rage" in the fall of '69, planned in '70 to blow up Columbia University's Lowe Library. But instead, they blew up the Greenwich Village townhouse that had their bomb-making factory in the basement, killing three of themselves. "Ain't that some shit," summed up my reaction when I heard the news.

Marvin Gaye would certainly capture my confusion and dismay with "What's Going On?"

No one I knew well came back from Vietnam messed up. But, of course, I heard stories of guys who did: foot missing, missing arm, fragments of a mind missing, too. What loving soul didn't cry at the thought of all the Vietnamese children whose lives had been scarred if not literally blown away.

Like so many others who hated that war, I felt a boost when the Supreme Court overturned Ali's conviction for his stand—"I ain't got no quarrel with them Vietcong"—refusing induction into the Army. What a hero he was to me and so many of my peers. He had made what seemed to us the ultimate sacrifice, risking his career for his convictions. Of course, it didn't hurt that Ali was so *fine*.

The day the "The Greatest" was freed from the threat of imprisonment was a much needed something to celebrate. Of course, sister Angela was not free, but jailed in Marin County, California, with no hope of bail, for having played a part—they said—in Black Panther Jonathan Jackson's disastrous attempt to spring some brothers out of jail. "Free Angela" fliers, buttons, posters whipped around the world, a world with millions mourning the deaths of Jimi Hendrix and Janis Joplin—both twenty-seven when, one month apart, they OD'd.

For those of us into the spirit of love, and peace, and aching for the world to be a better place '70 was a hard year. Many a day good news was hard to find. But it was there if you looked for it: in César Chavez and the United Farm Workers' first victory over grape growers; in the first Earth Day, Earth Week—with more and more of us recognizing how we had dogged our environment. Like Marvin, we were thinking "mercy, mercy, me," while the Beatles had a hit with "Let it Be."

And wonders never ceased: though Apollo 13 kerplunked, the Concorde had its first flight. And the World Trade Center was all the way up.

While I was trying to make sense of my world and find my place, I was singing quite a lot—at Lolly's, Mother's, Rush Over, Nero's Pit, and a bevy of other Northside clubs.

After The Shades of Black disbanded, Bonnie and I had gone our separate ways, pursuing divergent grooves. She linked with the rock band, Sweet Fire. For a time, I was with Lock and

Chain; for a time, with Lyfe, fronting with Gavin Christopher and a girl named Cheba. And there may have been some overlap in terms of my time with Lyfe and another group: The Babysitters, formed by four-hundred pound Baby Huey (né James Ramey).

The Babysitters' one and only album is a definite collectible, with "Mighty, Mighty" and "Hard Times" among the samples of their "psychodelized soul" featured on the LP, courtesy of Curtis Mayfield's Curtom label: *The Baby Huey Story/The Living Legend*. Only thing was, the legend never lived to see his LP hit the street. Baby Huey suffered a fatal heart attack in the fall of '70, a few months before the LP's release. I hooked up with the Babysitters shortly after Baby Huey's death.

With the Babysitters, I did mostly top forty stuff—a lot of Sly and the Family Stone, Aretha, Clapton, the Beatles, Santana, Ten Wheel Drive, Mountain. We did seven, eight shows a night with sometimes twenty-minute, sometimes just ten-minute breaks. We clocked out at about 3 A.M., by which time I had usually had my overfill of schnapps.

Some nights I had to be carried out to somebody's car. Some mornings I awoke not knowing how I'd gotten home.

Home was, at one point, a pad on the Northside, in a high-rise on Lincoln Avenue by the lake, which I shared with my friends Karen and Cheba. I had left my father's house a while ago, not long after he and Connie had their baby girl.

They named her Zaheva—"the Golden One" in Hebrew. I contributed her middle name, Aisha—"Life" in Swahili. Another baby in the family!

Connie was very protective of Zaheva. She was probably on pins and needles whenever Bonnie and I took Zaheva out. And she had reason to be, because we paid her no mind when it came to her prohibition on sweets. We'd walk the seven or so blocks to the candy store with Zaheva on my hip (and with her usually beating me up in the face, hitting pretty hard). We made sure she ate the candy we bought for her long before we returned home. Zaheva must have been about six months old when Bonnie and I booked because we were putting a strain on Connie's cool. Our wild ways—too-loud music, hanging out past midnight, sneaking boys into the house—made a bad fit now that she had little Zaheva and was herself mellowing out.

Bonnie and I bopped back to Mama's, where Bonnie stayed for a while. But Mama and I were not able to maintain, so I struck out on my own. Bonnie and I—no more Fric and Frac.

School was a balloon. I was just out there free-flying, playing it by ear, loving my independent living with Karen and Cheba. Cheba, in addition to being a fine singer, was also a witch.

She gave me a lesson in making magic when I had trouble with a Hispanic guy I was seeing—gorgeous long black hair, magnificent beard, luscious, big beautiful eyes, and a passion equal to mine for bike riding all around Chi-Town. Plus, he was an Aries, too.

We were going good until his estranged wife dropped into town with their two kids and he disappeared on me. *I was* PISSED!

"Light a white candle." That's how Cheba started the love-spell lesson. She told me to sit in the middle of the room and just talk to my man, tell him EVERYTHING I was feeling.

I lit the candle, I sat in the middle of the living room, I began talking to Borinquen.

Nature chimed in with a little ambience. A mighty thunderstorm kicked up as I talked to boyfriend. "You need to come see me" blah, blah, blah.

As I talked to him, sometimes my eyes were on the candle, sometimes on the raging rain. After about an hour, I got bored, and figured this mojo was going nowhere. I needed some fresh air.

I put out the candle, got myself suited up, and went for a walk in the rain. On the way home, I chilled a bit in a coffee shop around the corner from my place.

When I returned, the front door of our apartment was knocked down. There were black bicycle tracks all over our white rug. Cheba and Karen were hysterical.

"He was just here!" one yelled.

"He burst in," said the other, "he was looking for you! He looked like a mad man!"

I was more scared than impressed. And that was the last time I ever messed with white magic, black magic, gray magic, and with any other color witchcraft. Perhaps the spirit of Great-Gramma Bagby was telling me to leave that stuff alone.

I left Borinquen alone, too. He was out of my system when I hooked up with an Afro-Indian bass player with a lot of name: Ali Hassan Moy-din Shabu Genghis Khan. The Third.

Hassan Khan was a member of The Band of Gypsies, with a Mario, a Disraeli, a Bill, and Mario's girlfriend, Margo-of-the-purple-hair, whom we called "Sparkle Plenty." Along with Bill's girlfriend, Toosi (Mario's sister), they were all living in an apartment on East 67th. It was a commune of sorts.

After Hassan and I got close, I moved in with the crew and started living even more day-by-day. If someone had scored enough for breakfast in the morning—that was a wonderful thing. If not, our stomachs grumbled until someone begged, borrowed, or stole enough to satisfy us for the day—and for the night, often spent dropping acid or in a reefer cloud listening to Jimi Hendrix and Stevie Wonder and living life like so many other make-love-not-war types.

One of the things I loved about Hassan—he was good in bed, not that I had all that much for comparison. Plus, he loved to talk, and take late night walks in the park. And smoking grass and dropping acid and smoking grass and dropping acid and on and on.

Sometimes we'd ride a train line, tripping, spotting demons.

"That one's a demon."

"That one's *really* a demon!"

I suppose we were able to identify the hierarchy of demons. And angels? I guess the passengers we didn't spot as demons in disguise must have been angels by default.

At one point Hassan and I both went blonde. His straight hippie-hair, his mustache, his goatee—all blonde. My coif of choice was rather phallic: a fairly long stalk of Dippity-Do'd hair shooting straight up from the center of my head, with ringlets around the side of my face and along the back. My eyebrows were blonde too. I wore only black.

How did my mother react when she glimpsed me? Yeah, she thought it a bit morbid. "Why do you have to paint your nails black?" was one way she voiced her concern. But I didn't see much of her or the rest of my family those days. A time or two I dropped by for dinner, and a time or two my mother brought food by our pad.

I never sang with The Band of Gypsies, but Hassan and I jammed together a lot, just for fun. I went to his gigs and he went to mine.

Singing earned me about fifty bucks a night—unless I got docked. The Babysitters' bossman, Turk, was forever docking us for the slightest slip—being one minute late, making a tiny mistake on stage. And Turk flaunted the stuff he bought—new shoes, new shirt—with our docked money.

"Keep fucking up and I'll have a new wardrobe on y'all in a minute," he often quipped.

A time or two I snatched a little file clerking gig, once at NORC thanks to my mother. Sometimes I helped myself to five-finger discounts. With my 9 P.M. to 3 A.M. rush of weekend gigs, I sometimes sang steady for a two-month stint, sometimes, it was just two weeks. So, between that uncertainty and the docked singing wages, money was always tight.

From the time I started singing with Lock and Chain, and straight on through my Babysitter days, whenever I had a half-decent break or wasn't on a gig at all, I dug checking out other groups working the same circuit.

I believe it was sometime in '70, on a night I was working at Nero's Pit, that I stepped down the street to Rush Over to check out a group called Ask Rufus.

8

RUFUSIZED

Back in '66, some Illinois boys—guitarist Gary Loizzo, bassist Chuck Colbert, guitarist Al Ciner, drummer Lee Graziano—had come together for the making of Gary and the Nite Lites. About a year later, they changed up to The American Breed, cutting "Step Out Of Your Mind," for one. In '68, they had their chart-topper: "Bend Me Shape Me." By then, keyboardist Kevin Murphy was on board.

Some time in '69, itching to move on from teenybopper tunes, Al, Chuck, Lee, and Kevin spun off into a new group, eventually adding James Stella and Paulette McWilliams as lead vocalists. More personnel shifts came soon: singer, songwriter, and keyboardist Ron Stockert replaced James; bassist Dennis Belfield took over Chuck's spot.

The group had called themselves Smoke for a minute, and then settled on Ask Rufus, after a fishing and hunting column in *Mechanic Illustrated* magazine.

When I first caught Ask Rufus, the lineup was Al, Kevin, Ron, Dennis, and Paulette. And I was an instant fan. Here were these very adept white boys fusing Funk/R&B with Country/Rock, which is somewhere where I thought I lived. On another groove, they were doing something else that was very radical at the time: Ask Rufus was the first white band fronted by a black chick I'd ever seen.

What a stunning creature Paulette was—top-of-the-line black leather pants, fishnet tops (bottoms, too!), monster afro, eyelashes doing the Betty Boop. Guys came from miles away just to see her big boobs. And what a voice!—beautiful, strong. A very Sagittarius singer, and quite experienced.

Paulette had been singing since she was two and by age four, performing publicly (she could tap dance, too). At age eleven, she had been a winner of the Patricia Vance Amateur Hour. Plus, she had been doing jingles since she was in her early teens.

I idolized Paulette and we became fast friends, like sisters. She played a big part in my becoming me. I was tough-talking, tough-singing, but deep down I wasn't very secure about what I was doing. I was still ambivalent about a singing career. Part of me wanted to dream big on that score; part of me still thought maybe I'd find my bliss in a quieter, more solitary career: visual artist. But Paulette helped me build up the strength and conviction that maybe, just maybe I could make a life in music. It's because of Paulette that I got my first jingle gig (a commercial for Sears).

And remember Hassan? Had it not been for Paulette, I might never have met him. One day her fella, Howard, told her she had to meet his closer-than-a-brother friend, Hassan. And she did and then I did. Though there'd be plenty of days I'd wish she hadn't made that introduction!

Most of all, I had Paulette to thank for my becoming a member of Ask Rufus, when she decided to go solo in '72.

Paulette's decision put the group in a panic. How in the world were they going to replace her?

"Chaka," said Paulette.

The guys weren't wowed by the idea. They knew me as Paulette's friend but they had never heard me sing.

Paulette pushed. She even agreed to stay on for two weeks to work with me, help me master the material.

The guys agreed to give me a shot. After they heard me sing, they decided Paulette had been right. Did I want the spot?

Hell, yeah. Ask Rufus wasn't an autocracy like The Babysitters. Ask Rufus was a real *democratic!* band—everyone had a say. Everyone was really happy and free. I had longed to be a part of the group but had never had the gumption to lobby for inclusion.

Ask Rufus was a definite step-up—on average, maybe four shows a night. Plus, I made more money—not to mention way more interesting music.

We were performing at a club in the Chain-O-Lakes area, just south of the Wisconsin border, when Bob Monaco entered my life.

I say "my life" because most of the crew already knew him. Bob had managed and produced several groups—The Buckinghams ("King of Drag"), The Cry'an Shames ("Sugar N' Spice"). He had also worked with Breed, in the days following "Bend Me, Shape Me," when they were hard pressed to serve up another hit.

Bob and his partner, Jim Golden, teamed up with Breed's manager Bill Traut for the making of Dunwich Company and Arkham Artists. Producing the band Crow ("Evil Woman") was among the many things Bob had on his plate when he went to work on getting Breed–turned–Ask Rufus a record deal.

During a West Coast trip, Bob and Bill met with Jerry Weintraub, concert promoter extraordinaire—Elvis, Sinatra, Dylan, Zeppelin, The Beach Boys—and future movie producer (*Nashville; Oh, God; The Karate Kid*). The powwow was about Bob and Bill wanting to start their own label, to be distributed by RCA. And it happened. As Bob put it, "Jerry's influence was the magic." (They named the label Wooden Nickel Records, and one of their first hits was Styx's "Lady.")

In the meantime, Ask Rufus was swept away by a Chicago attorney, who got the group a deal with CBS—but the album was never released, due to artistic differences. As Kevin later explained to *Blues & Soul*, "There was a big row, because we thought [the producer Sandy Linzer] was just using us as a vehicle for his own machinations. You see, he wrote all of the material and we really didn't feel that it was in the direction that we wanted to go in."

By the spring of '71, Bob Monaco had relocated to Hollywood. About a year later, serendipity brought him back into Ask Rufus's life. In Chicago for a music trade show, Bob ran into Kevin, who brought Bob up to speed on the group. Kevin also invited Bob to check us out that night. A drummer who'd had a stint with Breed was by then part of that "us": André Fischer, who had also played with Curtis Mayfield and Jerry Butler. It's no exaggeration to say that André was born into music. He was the son of a singer (mother) and trumpet player (father) and nephew of keyboardist, composer, and arranger Clare Fischer, who would work with Rufus in the future. Also in the future, André would "marry music"—Natalie Cole.

Bob Monaco almost didn't "happen" the night we were playing at that Chain-O-Lakes club because he and his brother got lost en route to the club. When he later said they almost didn't make it to our gig—I wondered, what if he hadn't shown? Would my life have turned out differently? Then again, perhaps what's meant to be will be. But they did make it, in time to catch our last two numbers.

When Bob heard me, he flipped—"I thought I'd just heard the next Aretha Franklin, or the next coming of Christ. She floored me!" At the time, yeah, I knew I could sing but I sure didn't think I was all *that!*

Bob insisted on a demo, pronto. The next day, we hit it. That evening, Bob jetted back to L.A. to present us to RCA. They passed. But Bob was undaunted. He thought fast and he moved quick, calling up his friend Steve Barry, VP of A&R for ABC\Dunhill Records.

Barry was willing to give a listen, but Bob had to get to his office right away because Barry was about to hit the studio with the Four Tops.

Bob got there. Barry liked what he heard, and offered a record deal. When Bob told us the news we flipped!—then celebrated our butts off. (And it's my recollection that we got pretty messed up.)

I was nineteen. Age of majority was twenty-one at the time. I would need a parent to sign the contract. But I didn't want anybody to have anything to do with my business but me!

When I found out that a married woman was "legal" no matter her age, I had a powwow with Hassan. But first I had to get a parent to sign off on that!

"How are you going to support her?" my mother asked Hassan during her "interrogation."

When he told her his gig with the Staple Singers was steady, Mama was not impressed.

I pleaded with my mother to *please* let me marry.

"Absolutely not!"

About a week later, I lied and told her, "I'm pregnant, Mama."

My mother got us *quick* to City Hall. (Later, I told her I lost the baby.)

By then, my mother was back in the house on Carpenter Street, and had converted the basement into a rec room. When Hassan and I married, my mother went into overdrive, transforming the utility room into a bedroom, turning her basement into an apartment for us. She put a lot of work into it, but Hassan and I were hardly ever there. We preferred to vagabond, until we finally settled into a little apartment of our own on Jeffries.

Every other step of the way, we fought. A lot. I was working pretty steadily, bringing in all the money, and he was not really trying. At one point, I began to wonder if he was trying to pimp. I knew he had a couple of girlfriends on the side. And I had a feeling he had them to thank for the new bass guitars and other goodies he came home with. One day he had the nerve to sound me out about a plan of his: for him, me, and a chick named Brenda to live together—for his two women to be his money-makers. I was like, "Hell, no!" And we broke up. Not that it would last.

In the meantime, the group, which had trimmed its name to plain ole Rufus, had recorded at Chicago's Quantum Audio. Three singles: Ron's "Slip N' Slide," Al's " Feel Good" and Allen Toussaint's "Whoever's Thrilling You (Is Killing Me)."

I would never have chosen that last song because I still couldn't stand the blues. But when Bob brought the song to the table, he was adamant. "This is something you have to do, you gotta do it." So I went along, gave it my best.

Working in the studio—I was like a fish in water. It seemed so familiar, a feeling akin to coming home. For me, the big thrill was singing my own backgrounds at a time when vocalists stuck with the tradition of hiring backup singers.

For me, it wasn't a matter of frugality or the inability to find good backup singers. I knew how the background vocals should flow, so why shouldn't I do them? The guys were doing overdubs with their instruments. Once I got the hang of the recording technique, I asked if I could do my own overdubs, too.

"Whoever's Thrilling You" got mucho airplay and Rufus became something like famous in the Midwest. Our fame spilled over onto my little brother, upping his street cred. And I was so happy for him.

At school, on the block, people came up to Mark—"Hey, you really Rufus brother?" Some no longer introduced him as "This is my friend Mark," but rather, "Mama, this Rufus brother." The group really was a unit, as in the sum of the whole being greater than its parts. We weren't totally ego-free every minute, but we were truly a team. You could have called us the "Five Musketeers."

9

TELL ME
SOMETHING GOOD

We wouldn't be making our first album in Chicago. Bob Monaco just wouldn't have it. L.A. had better studios, better engineers, better talent, better everything, and Bob wanted only the best and better for us. So soon, we were California bound.

This wouldn't be my first time in L.A. A few weeks before Bob Monaco caught our act, Ike Turner had fallen in love with Rufus. He had flown us to L.A., put us up at Hollywood's Jet Motel, and said he wanted us to record in his studio. As it turned out, what Ike really wanted was for me to become an Ikette. I was like, *Hell, no!*, right along with the rest of Rufus. Ike had his brilliance, but he was in his insane days back then. Plus, I was really happy with Rufus.

But Ike's attention was certainly a boost. And I dug L.A. I came to dig it even more during the days we were out there working on our first album, *Rufus*.

We kicked it out pretty quick, adding to "Slip 'n Slide," "Feel Good," "Whoever's Thrilling You," three more songs by Ron, and four more songs by other people, including Ashford and Simpson's "Keep It Coming" and Stevie Wonder's "Maybe Your Baby." It all went so easy. But once we got out on the road and started working the stuff—that was a whole different thing. I had no idea how rough a promotional tour could be.

You're on the record company's dime, and they are determined to get their money's worth. They send you around to key markets where your first morning kicks off with a lot of phone or face-to-face interviews, followed by two or three radio station drop-bys for on-air chats with DJs, followed by maybe another interview or two, followed by getting ready for the evening gig, followed by the next day—rewind, replay—only the day might start earlier with you getting on a plane or train or bus bound for the next city, where you do more interviews, more visits to radio stations, more remembering to mention your "product" and the place you'll be gigging that night, more staying peppy as you answer some questions for the umpteenth time—*How did you get your start? Who are your influences? How do you classify your sound? What's the message in your music?* And every time, you have to answer as though you are hearing these questions for the very first time, as if the interviewer is original. You know he or she has to cover that ground, and perhaps also has to make a big deal over the fact that Rufus is an interracial band. Even though the only statement we ever wanted to make was that there were no limits to our creativity.

Young people generally don't get tired. And I had always been very high-energy, but out on that tour, for the first time in my life I was wiped out, stretched to the limit, stressed! There's precious little time to enjoy a city you've never been to before because there's precious little personal time. Especially in my case. The band was extremely overprotective of me. When they got a breather they could do what they liked—take off for some secret somewhere, pull chicks left and right—but don't even let a guy LOOK like he's going to say, "Hi" to me. And if I was some place where I had friends and I had time to chill with them in my room, when the rest of Rufus was ready to go to bed, they did a room check on me—put my friends out, made me go to bed. I had NOT signed up for four big brothers!

Ironically, some people very much *not* in the know assumed I was slippin-'n-slidin with the whole damned crew. Though there would come a day when I would get tight with one Rufus member.

My first album, my first tour, my first taste of what the music business was like—yeah, I was EXHAUSTED, but I was also so psyched. I was hungry for more. And I sure was glad I was living in music in '73. It kept me from getting too glued to all the bad news, all the chaos, conflicts, confusions, and debates—over Watergate, *Roe v. Wade,* The Yom Kippur/Ramadan War, the murder of Chile's Salvador Allende in a CIA-backed coup.

Okay, maybe I snickered a little when Spiro Agnew had to re-sign as VP after getting busted for tax evasion.

One thing that was certainly no laughing matter was the OPEC embargo coupled with the actions of SOBs at some American oil companies, which gave us jacked up oil prices, leading to long-ass gas lines, leading to fights at pumps, and si-phoning in the dead of night and, sometimes, even in broad daylight. I never realized how much everyday stuff was oil-based and oil-related until the prices of certain things started going up, up, up.

Of course, whether you were in L.A., Chicago, New York, or Whoville, whether you were conservative, liberal, libertarian, or politically non committal, you sighed a big relief when the news finally hit that U.S. troops were being pulled out of Vietnam. No more Vietnams! No more Vietnams! became my generation's mantra.

Looking back, and checking lists of old movies, I realized '73 was a pretty good year for flicks, too.

The Exorcist—killed me. I had read the book, and it had devastated me. At first I thought, no way was I going to see the movie. But I did, and I still haven't gotten over it. I still won't watch that movie again. True, I love horror, but it wasn't as if *The Exorcist* came out of the minds of two train-tripping fools spotting demons. *The Exorcist* was based on some real stuff.

The Sting—never saw it; *The Way We Were*—not my kind of movie; *Last Tango in Paris*—not my kind of movie; *The Harder They Come*—didn't see it; *American Graffiti*—not my kind of movie. *Serpico*—loved it, brilliant! *The Paper Chase*—

didn't see it; *Paper Moon*—that was cute; *Papillon*—Steve Mc-Queen was my boy! From *The Blob* to the *Magnificent Seven* to *The Great Escape, Love with the Proper Stranger, The Cincinnati Kid, Baby the Rain Must Fall, The Sand Pebbles, The Thomas Crown Affair, Bullitt*—I think I've seen every flick he made. He was a master at that rebel/loner-with-a-mind thing. *Papillon*, man—so psychological, so soulful, the most intelligent prison-escape movie I've ever seen.

Jesus Christ, Superstar? That's my all-time favorite rock opera. I still know all those songs because I ruined the grooves on that album from playing it so many times. For some reason that I can't remember I didn't see the movie until years after its release.

Like a lot of people I know, one thing I wish I could forget about the '70s—the fashion: double-knit polyester, leisure suits, platform shoes—yuck! But, you know, I still think the way we funkified our jeans with everything from embroidery to studs to rhinestones is cool.

Jeans were the mainstay of my stage outfits in the early '70s—jeans and gauzy Indian tops with mirrors. And the most bizarre platform shoes I could find!

Rufus didn't make a whole lot of noise saleswise. But we were hardly in shabby company. The Temps had their *Masterpiece*; Diana Ross, "Touch Me in the Morning": Aretha, "Until You Come Back to Me"; Paul McCartney and Wings, *Band on the Run*. Billy Preston's "Will It Go Round in Circles" and "Space Race"—now that I think about it, either one would have made a cool soundtrack for those first color shots we saw of Jupiter via *Pioneer 10*.

I didn't pout that *Rufus* came nowhere near a Grammy nomination, but you can bet I cheered when Stevie Wonder hit it triple: "You Are The Sunshine of My Life," Best Male Pop Vocal! "Superstitious," Best Male R&B Vocal and Best R&B Song! *Innervisions*, Album of the Year!

Was I daydreaming that one day I would be making my way onto the stage to accept a Grammy, to thank a river of people for all their love and support—mother, father, sisters, brother, Aunt Barbara, Aunt Kathy, producers, managers . . . Nope. I never *dreamed* Grammy. It was enough for me that ABC was keeping the faith. They were one hundred percent behind Rufus doing another album—this, when because of the oil crisis, the cost of vinyl was affecting the bottom line. Record companies got very particular about who could record. ABC was no different, putting a bunch of groups on hold. Rufus was among the ones who kept a green light. If that wasn't a vote of confidence, I don't know what was. Then, it got better.

We had attracted the attention of a manager with clout: Bob Ellis whose client's included Billy Preston and who had the cachet of being married to Diana Ross at the time.

"He saw something in us when we almost couldn't see it in ourselves," Kevin told *Blues & Soul*. "He first saw us do a set at the Whisky A Go-Go in Los Angeles, and he said he had to close his eyes because we were so bad visually—but he heard something in our music which he felt could be worked on."

Bob Ellis made a lot of things happen for Rufus—from opening for the Rolling Stones to gigging in Europe for the

Queens Jubilee for starters.

In the fall of '73, Rufus was at work on album number two, when I approached Bob Monaco about something on the top of my wish list: an original Stevie Wonder track on our album. By now, I was feeling free to dream big!

True to form, Bob went to work on working some magic. He had a connection to Wonder, and he used it. He got a copy of "Maybe Your Baby" to Wonder's ear.

But we didn't know that until the evening we were in the studio in Torrance, and Bob came in to say that Stevie Wonder was interested in showing us some new material.

"Yeah, right." And isn't that typical? How often we ask for things, pray for things, and then when the request is fulfilled, the prayer answered, we're like "Yeah, right." We all assumed Bob was pulling our leg, but we soon found out he wasn't.

There I was, in the studio with Stevie Wonder! Everyone was as gaga as I was.

We were ready, ready, ready when he launched into a tune. Then, after all that bated breath mode, and great expectations—what he came out with left us all cold.

"You got anything else?" I didn't mean to be rude. And obviously Stevie Wonder wasn't too put out, because he didn't get up and walk out.

"What's your sign?"

"Aries."

"Oh, well, here's a song for you."

The whole of his song was still in the ether. All he had was the hook. But it was enough. We all—the guys, Bob, me—we were like *Yeah!* over, as Bob put it, this "little ditty."

Next thing I knew I was working with Stevie Wonder on the lyrics for the "little ditty," which became "Tell Me Something Good." And because I was new and so jazzed about having some Wonder on our album, I forfeited a co-write credit.

A lot of people can't believe that. They ask me if I'm bitter. Did I feel exploited? If I had been able to predict the song would be a smash would I have done things differently? No. I'm not bitter. In a way, I was exploited, but that happens to everybody no matter what field you're in. We used to call it paying your dues. If I had known the song would be a hit— well, I couldn't then, couldn't later, and still can't predict a hit. In fact, the songs I most love are the ones that don't become hits.

But for argument's sake, had I known that song would be huge, I might still have done the same thing. I was young, yeah, and I was naïve about a lot of stuff in the music business, but I had sense enough to know a little something about "choosing your battles." Had I gotten all diva about it, who knows— maybe Stevie would have walked. Or maybe not. In any event, done is done. I'd be a fool to be stewing over the no-credit all these years later. It's really not my nature. That's one benefit of living in the moment: you don't much dwell on shit.

On the other hand, that approach can sometimes come back to bite you.

10

PACK'D MY BAGS

"How are we going to make a star out of you if you're going to have babies," scolded ABC exec, Otis Smith, when he found out I was pregnant.

"Listen, motherfucker, I'm gonna have babies AND be a star—with you or without you. How 'bout that?"

Don't get me wrong, Otis was our ace boon coon, he was getting good things done for us. But who was he to intrude on my biology?

It wasn't so much that I was hell-bent on superstardom. I just resented the hell out of his nerve—his insinuation that ABC would be the end-all be-all of any success I might have. And furthermore, that career trumped motherhood.

I understood where Otis was coming from. ABC no doubt

feared my having a baby might make me go soft on my career, and that it might also take a toll on my sexy quotient. I was determined to prove that such notions were hogwash. And like so many women then and now, I had to figure out a way to handle motherhood and career.

Turning what ABC saw as a negative into a positive was part of the impetus of my wearing low-cut pants and short tops—on and off stage—when I started to show. I was determined to celebrate motherhood and celebrate my belly, on which I sometimes painted stars, a moon, the sun.

I was over eight months pregnant when we recorded *Rags to Rufus*. Being with child was apparently not a hindrance. As André told one journalist, "I don't think Chaka realized it, but her voice was more forceful during that time. There must be some truth to that old saying that pregnancy can make you stronger."

Other than working with Stevie Wonder on "Tell Me Something Good," my most memorable moment in the making of *Rags to Rufus* was the creation of "You Got the Love."

> *You got the love*
> *Gimme the strength*
> *To keep on livin' yeah*
> *Whatever it is*
> *I can't do without*
> *What cha givin'*

The song just happened, when Ray Parker, Jr. popped up with

a song idea for me. When he started that guitar line—the words flowed like water. That song must have been written in all of ten minutes. Some of the best songs are the ones that come off the cuff.

Not long after we wrapped *Rags to Rufus,* I headed home to Chicago to have my baby.

Hassan and I had gotten back together, then broken up, then Rahsaan Morris entered the picture.

Philly-born Rahsaan had been a child when his family moved to Chicago. He spent a fair amount of time at the home of my mother's cousin Niecy, where sometimes on my visits he glimpsed me. Being three years older than me, he regarded me as a baby. He paid me no mind.

One night in '72, Rahsaan caught Rufus at the Chicago Theater and really dug us. The next day, when his friend Jerry told him that he and his girl Wendy (a friend of mine) were going to hang out with Yvette Stevens, he was down. He hadn't seen me—or so he thought—in years. He was speechless when we all met up and he realized that Rufus's lead singer was little Yvette Stevens. I didn't know this until years later. All I knew then was when my eyes locked with those of this tall, lanky dude, that was it—it was over. I was a goner.

Rahsaan and Hassan were like night and day. In Rahsaan I saw a man, a grown man. The fact that he was not some piece of ghetto trash (his father was a doctor) and he was educated (Dennison University in Ohio, where he majored in theater arts) held a lot of appeal for me: it meant intelligent conversation. Too, Rahsaan had a steady job: after threatening to sue for discrimination, he'd gotten into the Stage Union. Rahsaan also had this air of superiority going on, which I found a turn-on (as well as a bit of a challenge).

We were hot and heavy for a while and then broke up over some mail he really had no business reading. It was from some guy I'd met while on the road. He was a poet as it turned out. When he asked if he could send me some poems, my response was, "Sure." Rahsaan thought the poems were love letters.

And then I got on a merry-go-round: Hassan to Rahsaan to Hassan to Rahsaan. There was overlap along the way. I was clearly in a ball of confusion, some type of internal tug-of-war: part of me wanted stability, part of me wanted gypsy. It never occurred to me that I shouldn't have been in a relationship until I was clear about what I really needed, not what I needed in a man.

When I discovered I was pregnant, I was with Hassan, and a little perplexed. When I told Hassan I was pregnant, his take was, "Let's try to make this work." So when I returned to Chicago, I crashed at the apartment Hassan and I had called home.

I should not have been flying, of course, but I wanted to have my baby at home. Because I didn't look as if I was almost due, I was able to have my way. But at one point during the flight, I thought, *Mistake!* because—*Oh, no, am I gonna have this baby on the plane?* Thankfully, it was only pre-labor pains and I got to have my baby on the ground: December 21, 1973, via C-section, at Lying-in Hospital, where Mark and Tammy had been born.

During the pregnancy RESPONSIBILITY became my beacon. That's the biggest insight I had: that motherhood was a responsibility. And I'd had a strong feeling that the baby would be a girl.

When I held her in my arms for the first time I thought, now—*finally, at last*—I have someone who will mean more to me than anything in the world, someone I can be truly close to all the days of my life.

I named her Indira after a woman I admired, India's Prime Minister at the time; Milini (delicate in Hindi, and delicate she would be, as well as a bit of a hard-ass beneath it all); and Shobha, ("Shining" in Yoruba) because it sort of rhymed with Chaka. I and everyone else would end up calling her Milini. She'll reserve Indira for her stage name.

When I was back on my feet some people were shocked! appalled! that I still wore, on and offstage, low-cuts, letting all the world see my Caesarean scar. Ugly? How could a sign of bringing a life into the world be ugly?

Hassan and I had not been able to make it work. For one thing, I got the vibe that the good fortune I was having careerwise was grit in his craw. He had been hoping for a record deal long before I even imagined one. Too, what guy wouldn't get a little insecure over his girl working so close, so all-the-time with a band of nothing but guys?

After a few months back in Chicago, I decided that it had to be over, and that I didn't want him to be my baby's father. I told myself that since there had been some overlap with Hassan and Rahsaan, I couldn't be positive about paternity, I was free to choose my baby's father. Rahsaan, I thought, would make a better father than Hassan.

When I told Rahsaan I'd had a baby and that she was his, he stepped right up to the plate; he was ready to be responsible. Marriage? No, that wasn't part of the plan. And even though we never married Rahsaan would be a good father to Milini, forever a part of her life. I knew deep down that from the beginning, he had his doubts that Milini was his. When it came to Milini, Rahsaan was certainly one generous and understanding man.

He was also understanding when I told him that I was going to make L.A. my permanent home. It was the thing to do careerwise. Plus, I'd gotten hooked on no more wicked winter weather. I had had some twenty years of the Windy City. *Enough!*

In the spring of '74, I packed my bags. I eventually convinced my friend Toosi, who was enduring an abusive relationship, that she should pack her bags too (and those of her little girl, Kiki, my goddaughter). Toosi and I ended up sharing a place in L.A., near Doheny.

Not long after I shifted to L.A., Bonnie made the same move too with the man she'd had married in Chicago (Jesse Jackson had performed the ceremony!): saxman John Brumbach, who would work with Rufus, The Gap Band, and Parliament among other groups. Back in Illinois, John had kept the wolf from the door by building swimming pools, including handling any necessary demolition. That's how he caught the nickname "Boom." With her husband's nickname, Bonnie completed her stage name: Taka Boom.

Supergroovalisticprosifunkstication! Bonnie was never a Bride of Funkenstein, but she was on *Mothership Connection* (with Boom soloing on "P-Funk") and two other Parliament-Funkadelic albums. Bonnie also did a lot of session work with a bunch of bands, including Rufus, before joining Undisputed Truth. Then, the Glass Family. Then, going solo, with Mark and I doing back-up on her first album, *Taka,* which carried the hit "Night Dancin.'" That, in '79. By then, of course, a *whole* lot had gone on with Rufus.

11

KEEP IT COMING

Back in early '74, ABC, the Bobs, and all of Rufus were waiting for "Tell Me Something Good" to hit. As Bob Monaco has said, "Everyone just sat back and got their checking account deposit slips ready."

Come on, we had a Stevie Wonder song! ABC/Dunhill had gone all out in advertising that fact! And then, nada, bupkus. The sales were horrible. "Tell Me Something Good" was not an instant hit as some people think.

After three months, Bob was told to get another single ready for release. As I later found out, Bob was pretty depressed right around then. He started looking for another staff production job because, as he put it, "Producing is just like baseball, you only get three strikes!"

Then, chance and Bob's openness paid off—after he got some pretty mysterious encouragement.

Unbeknownst to me, while he was in Palm Springs playing in a music industry tennis tournament, Bob took in a show at a local club, where "The Amazing Kreskin" was performing. Like millions of others in America, Bob had seen Kreskin dozens of times on Johnny Carson's *The Tonight Show*.

At one point, something came over Bob. He thought, "What the hell?" He decided to ask The Amazing Kreskin if "Tell Me Something Good" was going to be a success. As Bob tells it:

They wrapped his entire face with Ace bandages, leaving only room for his nostrils and mouth. He had placed white gauze bandages over his eyes and it seemed totally impossible for him to read anything. The audience was invited to write any question on a small piece of paper and sign only their first name. So, I asked if Rufus and Chaka were going to be successful? All the questions were gathered up by one of his assistants and placed in a small fish bowl. He reached into the bowl, unfolded the note, and slapped it on his forehead, and after a few moments gave his finding. I watched and was amused by the entire game, always wondering, How could it be done?

When he placed my question on his head, after a few brief moments he clearly said, "Bob, 'Tell Me Something Good' by Chaka Khan and Rufus will exceed your wildest dreams of success." I was floored because I did not mention the title of the song in my note! My, My. Oh well, I thought, life goes on and this was just a freaky thing.

About a month later, on a Sunday morning in late April, Bob was playing baseball for Columbia Records Slo Pitch team, whose second baseman, Bobby Applegate (father of actress Christina Applegate), worked for Warner Brothers as a promotion man. (Lucky for us that Bob Monaco was into amateur sports!)

At one point, Applegate asked Bob about what was going on with "Tell Me Something Good." Bob was honest about how badly the song was doing, and then asked "Why do you ask?"

Applegate told Bob the program director of a new R&B FM station had heard Rufus and had asked him how he could get an extra copy of *Rags to Rufus*. Bob, Mr. Leave-No-Stone-Unturned, told Applegate that he'd get copies of the album over to his office the next day. Bob also told Applegate that anything he could do to help "Tell Me Something Good" get some airplay in the L.A. market would be greatly appreciated.

A few days later Bob got a call from Applegate: that DJ wanted fifty copies of *Rags to Rufus* for a station giveaway. He also wanted to meet with the execs at ABC Records.

Bob got on it. He—as Rufus later would be!—was so grateful to Applegate. Remember, Applegate worked for Warner! But his friendship with Bob and his love for *Rags to Rufus* enabled him to push industry politics aside. And that's how "Tell Me Something Good" got more and more airplay, and blew the lid off, zooming to the top of the charts, sending the album to gold. Last but not least, Rufus got its first Grammy.

How did I feel about that? I've gotten that question a lot over the years. My answer always disappoints: "I don't remember." I'm sure I must have been excited, but . . . What no memory of that landmark moment says about me, I'm really not sure. Was I high at the time? It's possible.

How do I feel about that song some thirty years later, when it's one of those songs I can't leave out of a show unless I want to get jumped? It's okay. It's light enough that I can have a little fun with it, you know, make it interactive, as in—"Okay, fellas, when I give the signal, sing, 'tell me something good,' with all the testosterone you can muster . . . and girls, you come in at your sexiest with 'tell me that you like it."

Being able to play with the audience makes doing that song over and over and over and over . . . less burdensome—unlike a song I will be get stuck with—a true ball and chain!—about a decade after "Tell Me Something Good."

12

ONCE YOU GET STARTED

When "Tell Me Something Good" hit, Bob Monaco said he felt as if he'd "been touched by the Angels."

By then, some members of Rufus had been touched by the green-eyed monster. The artwork for the *Rags to Rufus* truly groovy album cover featured a close-up of a denim shirt with our heads popping out of the pocket. Off to the side, there's a button with "Rufus" and bumping up against it another button inscribed "featuring Chaka Khan."

I'd be lying if I said I didn't get some thrill at the attention. But I also knew that what was thrilling me was killing the rest of Rufus. I knew some suspected I'd angled for a bigger share of the spotlight and didn't believe I was as upset as they were.

But I truly wanted us to be a group! I had nothing to do with that button and didn't crave being singled out. We had a good thing going and I didn't understand then why ABC would make a move that could very well create disharmony. Now I realize they singled out "the sexy woman"—it gave them a hook. It was marketing driven pure and simple.

We may have been almost-famous but Rufus was not so powerful that we could force ABC to rework the *Rags to Rufus* album cover. ABC was generally being really good to us. We didn't want to ruin it.

ABC went all out for *Rags to Rufus*, and we embarked on a tour—opening for Stevie Wonder—a tour that lasted damn near two years. I sometimes took Milini with me on the road; sometimes, I left her in Toosi's care; a lot of time, especially when I'd be away from L.A. for a significant number of days, I left Milini with my mother.

Being away from my baby was a killer. I missed her so! I felt some mix of guilt and anger when I thought about the daily, tiny, miracle moments of development I was missing out on. I think a big part of my drug thing was about escaping from those feelings. Too, there was the loneliness. Not only were the guys super-protective; I didn't have an assistant, wardrobe girl, or anyone like that back then to do sister-girlfriend stuff with me when I was on the road. Fueling the loneliness was not knowing who to trust. Over the years, I'd wonder if a guy was really with me for me or my fame. When in doubt get high. Over the years, I'd also get angry about all the mundane, simple shit that other people got for free—shopping without people gawking, true friendships, privacy—that I couldn't have. When angry, get high. Whenever I started feeling shit I didn't want to feel I got high.

The hectic pace—especially early on—also played a role. At times, getting high was the only thing that enabled me to unwind and go to sleep. Chamomile tea just didn't cut it.

And a lot of times I was just plain scared. I was still in some ways a child. The mounting celebrity, the applause, the screams of the fans, the more money than I'd ever dreamed of making— I didn't have a clue how to handle it all. And I had no mentor. I can't say I regret coming into success at an early age, but I caution young people so eager for fame and fortune—*yesterday!*— that "making it" later in life can be even sweeter—and usually more manageable because some wisdom has probably set in by then.

I had no clue back then. All I knew to do was stay in motion, stay overwhelmed. No wonder one night, in Texas, as I stood on the balcony of my hotel room, high up in the sky, I thought about just ending it—quitting the business, quitting my life. I was feeling so down, so trapped, but something— someone's prayer? an angel? some of Great-Gramma Bagby's "Soul Power"?—called me back to life.

In October '74, Rufus was back in L.A. on a break, but just from the tour—not from work. We had about a month to get it together on our next album *Rufusized*. By then, Al, Dennis, and Ron were long gone (and eventually got on board Three Dog

Night). They had let their pride get the better of them and split before "Tell Me Something Good" had a chance to become a hit. They just never got over the whole "featuring Chaka Khan" business. That hurt me to my heart.

The newcomers were guitarist Tony Maiden; Bobby Watson, who had worked with, among others, Rhythm Rebellion and Billy Preston; and keyboardist Nate Morgan, who had worked with Pharaoh Sander and Gato Barbieri.

Somehow, we got the album done and doing so was the start of my friendship with Brenda Russell. She was Brenda Gordon when she and Brian Russell got their song "Please Pardon Me You Remind Me of a Friend" on *Rufusized*, which also carried the song that became my anthem "I'm a Woman, (I'm a Backbone)" by Lalomie Washburn.

I teamed up with Tony and Bobby for "Somebody's Watching You"; with Tony and Kevin for "Right Is Right"; and with Tony for "Pack'd My Bags," with Rahsaan on my mind.

Me and the baby gonna miss you
I see your smile in her face
I only wish we were with you now
It's a lonely, lonely place

(And, yeah, around then Tony and I did do more than sing and write songs together).

The whole crew was in on the creation of the instrumental that became the album's title song. And it was my old Lyfe buddy Gavin Christopher who gave us "Once You Get

Started," which rocketed *Rufusized* to #1 and gold.

In the meantime, we were back on the road—grueling! grueling! grueling! But I knew there were singers who would kill to be grueled. And Aunt Barbara no longer had to fret about my baby fat. With the city-after-city, with the way I was dancing my hot-pants wearing, skimpified butt off on stage—I came close to looking like Olive Oyl. Grueling, grueling, grueling! And it didn't help any that Tony and I were mastering the Ike-and-Tina tango.

Tony and I were a disaster waiting to happen. We fought a lot, most often backstage after a gig. He seemed locked into that Gemini-perfectionist shit. He was never happy, always unsatisfied with the caliber of the whole group. And it wasn't long after he joined, that he emerged as something of the leader of the group. You would have thought Kevin would take that role. He was, after all, the one who had been with the group the longest, the only original member. But Kevin was very laid back, very to himself, never one to make any waves.

I think because I was the only girl in the group, I got the brunt of Tony's rage. Plus, we are all much quicker to take stuff out on the people we say we love.

So Tony would barge into my dressing room to rant about something that—in his mind—had gone very wrong during a set or an entire show—the way somebody played, some change of timing, the way someone hit a note or didn't hit a note.

He was such a yeller. In part, I think, because, while he had a lot to say, he wasn't very articulate. (I used to do a lot of talking for him during interviews, finishing his sentences, which, now that I think about it, must have pissed him off.)

"Tony, tell me exactly what it was that you didn't like about the gig?" I tried not to yell back.

"You know! You know what I mean!"

"No, I don't know what you mean."

Then he'd get even angrier and louder, and then I'd get angry and loud, and then things escalated to the point that back-up singers or band members ended up pulling us apart. Tony and I tore up many a dressing room. I remember our doing particular damage at Circle Star in San Francisco where we played often. (And my relationship with Tony made me decide I'd NEVER again have a boyfriend I worked with—only I forgot about "never say never.") But I have to say, when we weren't fighting Tony and I made some wonderful music together. The whole group did.

Going through clippings from my glory days with Rufus, brings back strong memories of how different the group was at the time—what a true phenomenon, and how people kept trying to figure us out, put us in a slot. As I told a writer for *Soul*:

We are rhythm and blues oriented for the most part. But we really are more versatile than we are one thing. Being placed in a category has brought about a lot of trouble for the group and it restricts you to one market. It's an interesting thing. A Black band is always labeled an R&B band and white band is labeled Rock. Now music is everything and everything is music and there should be no distinction and that distinction is coming off a color thing and that is really sad.

"Krudde." That's what we had started calling our music in our effort to get people to back off the need to pigeonhole us. "Music that is below the belt, way down, real deep." That's how Nate explained it to the *Soul* reporter. "We're going to spread Krudde," Nate proclaimed, "not only in L.A. But everywhere we play." Tony coined the term. He was forever talking in his own terms. During a practice session, if a groove wasn't right—"It ain't got no hubba!" Tony might say. And when it came to our music—"Krudde."

To me "Krudde" was something really fringy around the edges, not really pure, but definitely strong.

We were at Whisky A Go-Go the night before Doris Elkins interviewed us for *Black Stars* magazine.

After spending time with these six talented musicians, it does not take long to realize that Rufus is a group of humble, beautiful people who have paid their dues and are seeking to reach their star; to twinkle for a while. They are quick to pay tribute to those who have helped them along the way, like Bob Monaco (their producer) who allowed them freedom to arrange and record their material in addition to making creative changes without feeling threatened or hassled.

When I look back, I'm amazed at how something like pure we were, idealistic, and open. We really were less into fame than we were into the freedom to be creative. We wanted our art to be the star.

As André put it, "We're minstrels, so to speak. We carry a message, not a supreme message, but simply a means of expressing ourselves to others. After all, music is communication. We don't like unhappy songs. We don't like unhappy things. We like songs that make people happy, because we're reflecting in our music, how we *want* things to be."

Yeah, we were happy alright. And we spent a lot of time and cash "getting happy."

Sometimes I wonder. If I had only been into natural highs, would I ever have hooked up with Richard Holland at all? We wound up spending some six years together.

13

HAVE A GOOD TIME

Richard had been a bit of a fan before we met. He had crisp memories of driving along in his VW Bug, playing *Rags to Rufus*—singing out loud to his favorite cut, "Smokin' Room."

Ain't sayin' I'm right
Ain't sayin' I'm wrong
Ain't sayin' there's any such a thing as short or long
It seems you been here many times before
It's too beautiful but true
And I'm glad I got the chance tonight
To share my now with you

Richard *loved* that song. He played it over and over again

(probably on an eight-track tape!). When I hit the high notes, "it just drove me crazy," he said.

In a way, Richard's adoptive parents brought us together. Mildred and famed jazz percussionist Milton Holland owned my cute little bungalow rental in the artsy enclave of Laurel Canyon. (Toosi and I had had a serious falling out and decided being housemates wasn't going to work. For help with Milini, I took a nanny, Sheila, who would work days and anytime I needed her to stay overnight.)

Naturally, Richard's parents told him I was their tenant, in the house two doors away from the one in which he was living. And one day Richard knocked on my door.

"Hi . . . my parents own this house and if you ever need anything, just knock."

About an hour later, I took him up on his offer. "Got any weed?" He did.

Not long after that, I was back, asking if he wanted to come along to a Stones concert at the Forum.

I clicked quick with this cute, long-haired guy with a great sense of humor, and, as I soon discovered, some truly cool tattoos. He had music in him, too. He had played guitar for years, working it at various clubs around town. But music was not his primary passion. He had studied film in college. His big hope was for a career in film. He was working at Universal, in independent film acquisition, when we met.

We went from friends to lovers in no time at all, and were constantly together. He was there during my gigs. He was there after my gigs, too, when I needed to cool out at an after-hours spot. Sometimes, I'd on-the-cuff pair up with a piano player and jazz away. "I Wish You Love" was one of Richard's favorites.

Richard and I curled up with Hesse, Camus, Carlos Castaneda. We had long conversations—and debates!—about the books we read. We both loved horror—we read Stephen King together. Practically each new movie that came out—in any genre—we saw it. Old flicks, too. Richard was a walking encyclopedia when it came to film. And he was convinced that everybody else—including me—should know everything he knew. He inspired me to read up on the old Hollywood scene. Richard really respected my mind; he loved my thirst for knowledge, my yen to keep learning.

Sometimes, when I was into one of my ink drawings, he was into one of his big oil portraits. And, no, the parallel with my parents was not lost on me. Even *I* got that one!

Richard laughed at my pre-dawn jones for a jelly and hot sauce sandwich. He loved my mac-and-cheese. We were forever going out for the best steak dinner in the world, at Dantana's in West Hollywood, a habitual hangout for Belushi, De Niro, and other Hollywood heavies. Richard and I became friends with Dantana's mâitre who sometimes "closed" the restaurant at 1 A.M., but let his special guests party on.

In Jacksonville, Florida, while touring with the Stones, Richard and I snatched a little time to frolic on a beach at night when we were a little too tipsy. He got it into his head that his mission at that moment was to charge into the water and fight a shark. And me, I got it into my head that my mission was to run in and save him. The fact that I wasn't a strong swimmer didn't matter because I tripped and smacked my head on a rock before I could drown! We somehow got to an emergency room for stitches and a future scar on my forehead.

Richard was bleeding too. Frictions had begun to surface. Our frolic on the beach had included a fight, though neither of us will remember which came first—our fight or his charge for the shark. And what was that all about? That's easy. We had just seen *Jaws*. Richard had a habit of truly getting into every film he saw. After seeing *Chinatown,* he even bandaged his nose.

When Rufus had a gig in Honolulu, Richard and I managed to remain injury-free. I got in a lot of much needed R&R, lying on the beach, chilling on a Catamaran ride. Richard learned to surf.

Now and then, we managed a true get-away: a trip no-way, no-how connected with my work. One of our firsts was to Puerta Vallarta, a place we returned to often. We also went frequently to San Francisco, for the Renaissance Fair. When we went, we often took Milini, who had warmed to Richard. He, in turn, grew to treat her as if she were his child. (Milini, who would sometimes spend summers with Rahsaan, would forever regard him as her daddy.)

Fired by his childhood fascination with *Treasure Island,* Peter Pan, and Gauguin, we once found time for a trip to Tahiti. He *loved* it. I *hated* it—I hardly left the hut. Thank goodness, I'd brought along a couple of books.

No phone. No TV, which I need—it's my background

music! No electricity. Plenty of mosquitoes. Lots of food (that's Club Med for you).

All there was to do was eat and eat and eat—and do water sports. And Richard was a water freak. Scuba diving, surfing, snorkeling—the whole nine yards. Not me. I've always had a respect for the ocean, but no desire whatsoever to bond with her. I'd read articles about the waterworld in *National Geographic* and elsewhere. I knew just enough about what lurked in the deep to not be interested in making any sea creature's acquaintance.

My only magic moment occurred during the flight to Tahiti. The plane was so high—"Look!" Richard poked me—we could see the curvature of the earth. "Wow!" Richard and I experienced a lot of Wows together.

We also experienced plenty of true friendship times, at a restaurant or at dinner at our house (we loved to barbecue!), with people who didn't want anything from us or from me: people who weren't there to get high, steal, lie about how close we were, or in other ways waste my time—people who didn't epitomize the song Dave Wolinski and André Fischer crafted for *Ask Rufus*:

> *Painted faces, sunburnt skin*
> *Fixed expressions, smiles worn thin*
> *Caught in the blink of neon of Hollywood*
> *Bending battles, maneuvering schemes*
> *False expressions, washed up dreams*
> *Everybody makes believe*

In Hollywood, Hollywood

People, people, people—I too often had a hard time saying no to people because—I don't know, maybe I had (have?) some kind of complex or something—some need to be loved, to be liked, not to displease, to make people feel alright even if they are no good for me, a drain on me.

Richard's old band-mate, Charlie Villars; Richard's since-high-school buddy, Scott Enyart and his wife, Nancy; and Stephen Bishop. These were some of the trusted, safe souls. With them, Richard and I had really good times: a lot of pure clowning around. In addition to being a great singer-songwriter, Stephen was such a comedian! As was Richard. (And it was Richard who arranged for me to be on Stephen's first album, *Careless,* where I did the duet "Little Italy" and sang back-up on "Save It For A Rainy Day.")

But the quiet times, the safe times, the times where life was something like normal—with breathing room—were so few, too few because most times it was show-time—in studio, on a stage, many stages, one stage after the other with me in one of my, as one journalist put it, "Queen-of-the-Stone-Age" outfits or some variety of my feathers-and-leathers. Bob Ellis had triggered the new look.

"What part of yourself would you like to explore?" he had asked.

I'd long ago dug deep into my African heritage. Bob's question got me thinking about checking out my Native American heritage. My mother's paternal grandmother and Great-

Gramma Bagby had had a heavy measure of Blackfoot blood.

I also had Bob Ellis to "thank" for those big red lips on our fourth album *Rufus Featuring Chaka Khan*, which aside from the lips is most remembered for yet another song Tony and I teamed up on:

> *You are my heat*
> *You are my fire*
> *You make me weak with strong desire*
> *To love you chile my whole life long*
> *Be it right, or be it wrong*
> *I just want to satisfy ya*
> *Though you're not mine*
> *I can't deny ya*
> *Don't you hear me talking baby?*
> *Love me now or I'll go—*

By then, I was no longer so crazy about my look.

"I'm tired of the feathers-and-leathers," I told a writer for *Circus* magazine. "I'd like to wear some fabric for a change. I'd like to be Eastern looking—it could be tight-fitting and very little of it, maybe Arabian and Egyptian all mixed up."

I sure was.

"I'm having a silver head-dress made up now, with two real bird wings on it, like a Mercury's skull, the messenger. We may be working with fashion designer Stephen Burrows on the concept. I'd rather wear things that people in the audience can't wear, but that they'd like to wear. You've got to stay one step ahead." Now I wonder, *Why?*

I had put myself out there as a sex symbol with no thought of the consequences: the negative ideas people would develop about me (all body, no mind); the photos and videos of me that would embarrass some members of my family, and leave my children open to ridicule.

Today, I am so happy to sing in a simple outfit (with my buns covered)—all black my preference. But back then, I had gotten caught up. I had made that slide from artist to entertainer. My voice couldn't possibly be enough. Rufus was an act, and once you get started with that—especially if you're a success—your manager and your record company will thrash you if you try to change up. Not that I'm laying blame. As my remarks to that writer reveal, I was really into "the act." And the more outrageous and outlandish the better.

No wonder we ended up attracting people who would rather act up than listen to our music. The writer for *Circus* captured the chaos when he wrote:

Onstage . . . Rufus's brand of fiery funk has been so hot recently that concert after concert has been halted by the unruly crowds. Tony Maiden doesn't get a chance to stretch out on any solos. Chaka doesn't get to run through her whole repertoire. At one point this spring, the band couldn't hear themselves playing for six straight weeks. Again, and again, as at Shea stadium, nervous promoters have ushered Rufus off the stage before the act is really finished.

Have we become freaks? This wouldn't be happening if I was doing my deeper love: jazz, if . . . When I was interviewed back then, I camouflaged.

> "We probably don't need to know more than three or four songs . . . including the encore," Chaka jokes, making light of the puzzling situation. "The audience never lets us get past that. One night at the Spectrum in Philadelphia this guy was running around shooting the lights out. There were waves of people swarming all around, and for a while we couldn't figure it out. . . . What a strange effect we're having on these people. I don't worry about crowd control, though . . . They paid their money, they can do whatever they please. I remember when I used to go to concerts I liked to get rowdy too. If they want to act like damn fools, I'll leave. See the thing is to know when to leave, that's the key to survival.

It's always so much easier to be cavalier than philosophical, and actually think about the consequences. What if someone had gotten shot? Trampled? Stomped? Would I have really not felt any guilt over that? Hindsight and incidents such as the stampede at Chicago's E2 in February '03 that resulted in twenty-one deaths and scores of injuries when security sprayed mace and the crowd gave way to mass panic—that stuff makes you think! And then, a few days later in Providence, Rhode Island, that horrible, death-dealing fire sparked by the pyrotechnics Great White used during their show at The Station—that kind of stuff gives you some serious 20/20!

But back in the '70s, I didn't want to care about things like that, and it was so easy for me not to care, because I was one of those people who hardly ever knew when to leave a party, and who sometimes forgot to allow enough time to elapse between when I "got happy" and when I had to be on stage.

Yeah, I had trouble coping. With the demands and pressures of career. With being a single mother. And there was all the weird shit I was attracting because of my act—guys obsessing, sending me sick fan letters. At one point, even somebody I knew came out of the woodwork all crazy.

I don't know if he was really an Albino or if he just looked like one. He was someone I'd known from my days at Calumet High. He had a little crush on me back then. Though the feeling wasn't mutual, we used to speak. After I got "famous," he somehow found my number and never stopped calling. To tell me how much he loved me, of course.

The phone calls got a bit much. He'd call odd hours of the night, so sometimes I left the phone off the hook. What else could I do? We didn't have answering machines back then, so there was no such thing as screening calls. If I forgot to take the phone off the hook and happened to pick up—he talked and talked.

Change my phone number? Yeah, I did that. Somehow he got the new number. He had the record company's number too, and he called, called, called there, too. I kept hoping he'd just get tired. I couldn't bring myself to sic the law on him—until he threatened to bomb ABC/Dunhill. That's when I called on one of America's oldest security outfits, the Pinkertons, for an up-coming concert in Chicago.

Security had a photo of the guy. When he showed up, they nabbed him. I didn't press charges because all I wanted was for him to leave me alone. The scare the Pinkertons gave him, thank goodness, was enough.

"If you remembered everything you did," a friend once said, "you would kill yourself." I don't know about that. But I am a little glad that I don't remember everything. But, of course, others do. Like David Nathan, who recounted a "less-than-satisfactory performance" in his book *Soulful Divas*.

It was early '76. We were playing at the Forum. It was Nathan's birthday and our concert was something of a birthday present to himself. There he sat, "preparing to watch Rufus and Chaka blow the roof off of what I expected to be a dynamite show," but—

> Chaka was clearly in "outer space," and every time she
> would attempt to begin singing, she would literally knock
> over the microphone stand! Another group member
> would pick it up, and within a minute or two, Chaka had
> knocked it over once more. She was incoherent on some
> of the tunes, storming through songs and barely commu-
> nicating with the audience. It was as if we weren't there.
> And while other band members tried to compensate with
> their sterling musicianship, Chaka was the center of atten-

tion—and the audience wasn't happy. This was my first clue that she just might not be handling life and success at the top quite as easily as she'd made out in our interview, and that she just might have resorted to different methods to deal with the pressures of the music business.

The interview David Nathan referenced had taken place three months prior, in Bob Ellis' office on Sunset Boulevard. Nathan confessed that he had "expected to meet the wild outrageous fiery performer I'd seen in the few Rufus shows I'd attended." Instead, he found "a reflective, intelligent, thoughtful young woman."

I talked with him about how critical it was for Milini to be happy. "So I've got to be happy, too." I talked about wanting to have two more children, wanting to be financially secure for their sake, wanting to get to a point where I could "pace myself out and have the time for myself that I need." I also talked national and world issues—other people's problems that concerned me—and about the possibility of my getting "into a position where maybe I might want to stop singing and go into another career where I can do something about the things that need changing."

What are you contributing? That was a thing that dogged me a lot. I was giving people some good music, but I never felt that was enough. So why didn't I stop and become a fulltime agent of change? For the same reason some lawyers work ninety hours a week. Work can be addictive, too. And when the money is good, it's not that easy to walk away. I know some have done it. I could not. Too, my singing was the only part of myself I was secure about. It was the only place I felt at home.

As my performance at the Forum revealed, when it came to things in the world that needed changing, I needed to first make some changes in my own world.

14

BETTER DAYS

It took some doing to get divorced from Hassan. He'd become a rolling stone; I had a hell of a time tracking him down. But eventually I did. And he signed the papers. So when Richard popped the question, I said, "Yes!"

We were in love. I was sure it would be an everlasting love. Richard thought so too, and he was hoping marriage would help us cut back on the craziness.

In the spring of '77 we did the I-Do. It was a fairly large and fabulous affair at Richard's parents' place. Richard's mother had been eager to do a big-deal thing (and they could afford it!), so I let her have her way and handle the whole shebang.

Richard's parents were of Jewish ethnicity. When it came to religion, they were atheists. Richard, agnostic. Me? Uncommitted. But somehow we ended up with a Rabbi and a pretty full-out Jewish wedding—I stepped on the glass and everything.

And I didn't get married in some Wild Child outfit. I went for simple and elegant: an off-white chiffon gown (that cost a small fortune); my hair up in a bun; around my head, a ring of flowers. My look was a little Medieval. (I was under the influence of the Renaissance Fair.)

As for the wedding guests, we had some of every kind of person, from little old yenta-type ladies to Right on!-Right on! type brothers to flower-power leftovers to a couple of my freaky friends, with whom Richard caught his mother smoking weed.

My own mother hadn't cared for Richard from the first moment they met, during one of my trips home to Chicago. And she had not been pleased when I told her I was going to marry. Still, she came to the wedding (with Gramma Maude) but she was not a happy camper, especially after Richard's father, at one point, asked, "Who's going to give her away?" And Richard's mother shouted back, "Oh, you can do it."

My mother wasn't the only person displeased about the marriage. A lot of people took issue with our bliss. We got hate mail, snide remarks, killer glares. When Richard answered the phone one night he heard, "I'm gonna kill you." The caller was a drummer of note, who was just too through that this white boy had me. Funny thing is, years later he had nothing but warm embraces for Richard whenever their paths crossed, claiming no memory of his crazy call.

Another musician—unfortunately blind and unfortunately not color blind—didn't threaten to do Richard bodily harm but he did let him know in no uncertain terms that he was triple pissed. Then, one day Richard could only laugh when he ran into this guy at a party, with a white woman on *his* arm.

"Dude," said Richard, "You know the girl you're with is white?"

Jet magazine proved it was doing its due diligence by captioning some photos of us with: "Chaka Khan and her husband, Richard Holland, who is a white man." Heaven forbid readers mistake him for a very light-skinned black man. And it's ironic because Richard, part Italian, part Mexican, could easily be claimed a person of color. But that didn't matter to many. What mattered was that he wasn't black. That I was not white was an abomination in the eyes of many whites, we saw without their saying a word, especially whenever a tour took us South.

The crap we caught as an interracial couple was the least of our troubles. Marriage did not make us curb the craziness. When Richard wasn't drunk or otherwise high, we fought about *my* doing so much drugs. He feared I'd kill myself. He wanted no more repeat performances of having to call an ambulance, having to endure the anxiety of waiting to find out if they'd pump my stomach in time.

It had happened before we married, at the end of a two-day recording binge. To compensate for the lack of sleep we had all been doing a lot, a lot of coke. When I finally got home, finally able to get some zees, naturally I couldn't sleep. I thought maybe some music might help, so I put on, I think, some Billie Holiday, some Ten CC, and some somebody else. The music didn't do it.

I had some Placidils, so I took one. When nothing happened quick enough for me, I took another one. It had been hours since I'd eaten anything. What happened next—I don't remember, but Richard sure did.

According to him, I managed to make it to his house where I collapsed. When he saw my pulse was faint, he called the paramedics. They pumped my stomach in the ambulance.

The thing I most remember about being in the hospital was some caseworker coming at me with dumb-ass questions.

"Are you under stress?"

Oh, no, being famous, working overtime—stressful? Nah.

"Is your daughter making it so difficult for you . . . that you want to hurt yourself."

I don't know how she got the idea I was a failed suicide.

"Do you—?"

"Get the—" Well, never mind. I'm sure you can imagine my response.

My drugging and Richard's drinking were not the only stressors on the marriage.

There was the tension with Rufus: the guys didn't like Richard. There was the tension with my mother: she and Richard it seemed would never get along. And Richard had some serious issues with my father. He thought my father was ripping us off, and he knew my father sometimes supplied me with drugs. One time, when Richard confronted my father about it, Daddy went after him with a baseball bat. There were times I felt like the rope in a tug-of-war.

The demands of career were a stress on every aspect of my life: the traveling, the gigs, the photo shoots, the interviews, the time, time, time—minutes . . . hours . . . days given over to career, all of it eating away at quality and quantity time with Milini, with myself. Believe me, I know some people won't exactly weep for me; but when you've developed the problems I had, you can't put anything before your addiction, let alone family before career.

This crazy life of mine inspired Richard to "Better Days":

We've got better days
There'll be better days
We've got better days

I wanted to believe in better days too. I wanted to stop getting high. I wanted to be a responsible mother. I wanted some slow-down, some order in my life, some help with coping. That's why I asked my mother to pack her bags.

"What can I do to get you here? I need you. I don't want anybody else watching my baby." Soon, I had Bob Ellis on the phone helping me convince Mama to move to California.

"Whatever we can do to get you here, we plan to do it," Bob said. "We want to get you a house—would you come if you had a house and a new car and you wouldn't have to work anymore?"

Mama was thinking this was one of those too-good-to-be-true type situations. She knew showbiz is risky, fickle. After years of moving—in her never-ending quest to "upgrade"—she had finally settled in at a great property in South Shore, where she planned to live for the rest of her days. It was on a large lot and consisted of a low-rise apartment building and, behind it, a five-bedroom house. (Indeed, my mother was every bit the money-managing maven that her mother was—a talent I certainly did not inherit.)

Once again, the property was a family affair: Barbara and her sons, Amaechi and Elkanah (from her second marriage), lived in the house. Mama converted the top two apartments in the other building into one apartment for her, Tammy, and Mark. In one of the downstairs apartments, lived Aunt Kathy and her son, Dwayne; in the other, Gramma Maude and Great-Aunt Anna Mae. (Great-Gramma Sallie had passed.)

Are you crazy? That's how most of my mother's family and friends reacted when she told them I had asked her to move to L.A.

I knew Mark would be down with the move. He was coming up on seventeen and had come into an aptitude for the bass. I knew he'd love nothing more than to be up close on the L.A. music scene.

But my mother feared Tammy, almost nine, might have trouble adjusting, might be heartsick about leaving her three best friends, her cousins and neighbors.

In the end, my mother relented. In the summer of '77, with

Mark and Tammy in tow, she made the move and started scouting for a house, while I was on the road. And so, did I buy my mother a house as I'd vowed to as a child? Essentially, yes. My mother was always a smart cookie. I did what needed to be done for the down payment and to secure the mortgage, and we agreed on a salary for her services—watching Milini chief among them—that would allow her to pay her mortgage. She was wise enough to know there could be confusion if the deed remained in my and Richard's name, so it wasn't too long before the house was transferred into her name.

I was right about Mark. Almost immediately he started doing his bass-thing at little clubs around town, and much to my mother's chagrin, dropped out of high school.

And my mother was right about Tammy. The move was very traumatic for her. She missed her cousins so! But in time, Tammy adjusted, settled in. And didn't I spoil her to death with frequent shopping trips, and celebrity thrills, such as meeting my friend Natalie Cole.

Natalie and I had gotten to know each other in the summer of '76 in LAX. We were both headed to Japan for work. There, we did a duet on a Tokyo TV show. And we got close. You bet it was very special to meet the daughter of Nat King Cole, but I wasn't into having a friendship with Natalie because of who her father was, but because of who she was—a beautiful spirit.

Tammy was in seventh heaven when I took her along to Bob and Diana's house—she couldn't believe she and Milini were in the pool with Diana Ross's kids!

After awhile, Tammy stopped daydreaming of being back in

Chicago. She came to love California, except for the times she and my mother had to hightail it to my rescue—Richard's rescue, our rescue—down near Malibu.

Richard and I had moved there in the fall of '77, around the time my mother moved into her perfect never-need-to-upgrade-again! L.A. house. She had chosen that house in large part because it was close to where I was living. And then, *blam,* I ended up moving some thirty or so miles away. Since Richard had been the one who wanted to move and had picked out the place, yeah, the plot thickened between him and Mama.

It was really a gorgeous place: a sprawling ranch, atop Magic Mountain in Calabasas.

It was beautiful. A six-bedroom Spanish style house, with a waterfall in the back. A swimming pool with a cantina. A huge bedroom with boulder walls. To further the "wilderness" effect, Richard even bought a shotgun, and had it mounted on the living-room wall.

We had chickens, ducks, geese, rabbits, a couple of dogs, a horse we named Equus, a pygmy goat (Timmy) and other animals.

Some friends and family thought Richard was working overtime to control me, isolate me, be my Svengali. Richard would say he was trying to put some distance between us and the madding crowd—trying to help slow it down, slow it all down, ease up on the pace, get us to turn to nature instead of drinks and drugs for escape.

Didn't work. There I was in this atmosphere of paradise, with the animals. And I'd loved animals as a child. Remember

Mimi?

Before her, when Daddy was home, I had other dogs, a cat or two, and parakeets for a time. I don't know if I had a natural-born love for animals or if it was an acquired taste because I wanted to be like Daddy and love whatever he loved. Next to music, animals had been his passion as a boy. He, who had so little, thought nothing of taking in a dog he happened upon. He'd just improvise—a belt or piece of rope for a leash, any old piece of dish for a feeding bowl. With so little parental supervision, at one point, he had turned his home into a menagerie: dogs, rabbits, golden hamsters, pigeons tethered to the windowsill, fish in the bathtub.

The fresh air, the space, the peace and quiet, the "therapy" that comes from caring for animals—I couldn't go all the way. I just wasn't into no Green Acres shit. And Richard and I couldn't find balance. We became Sex-Drugs-and-Rock-n'-Roll clichés.

We didn't have goals or ponder things like "purpose." We felt our purpose in life was to indulge ourselves. We ran through money as if it really did grow on trees—for two Mercedes convertibles (mine yellow; his black), a Jeep, one of the last Volkswagen Beetles, thousands and thousands of dollars worth of clothes from Maxfield Bleus, original art work, drugs, liquor, some exotic animals—snakes, owls, black widows, tarantulas—and all that came with keeping them and all the other animals, the whole damn ranch.

But the things never, of course, satisfy; things never make your problems go *Poof!* How in the hell could two people who were so well-read, two people who prided themselves on their quest for knowledge, not know that?

Then again, I was never one to get attached to things anyway. I was constantly giving things away, or shrugging it off when someone ripped me off. I lost things, too: my diamond and ruby engagement ring, for one. I don't know where or how but one day it was—*Poof!*

Another time, Richard asked after a show, "What happened to your bracelet?" It was an exquisite silver and turquoise number he had bought me. On an impulse, I had tossed it into the audience.

My "carelessness" was another thing Richard and I fought about—in front of Milini, unfortunately, letting history repeat itself. And when I called up Mama in tears during or after a fight, she hurried down, bringing Tammy. It really messed my sister up to see me such a wreck, crying, crying, crying.

One thing Richard and I never argued about was my cutting back on the leathers-and-feathers and the attendant outrageous aspects of my act. He had long felt it distracted from my voice, a voice whose sophistication never received adequate showcase he thought. The simple red dress I sport on *Chaka* (the album cover shot by our friend Scott) was in part a result of his influence, as was my decision to test the waters with a solo album.

Richard was all there when it came to my desire for freedom. The truth was, I was fed up with democracy. What would it be like to do only the songs I wanted to do? Besides—

"Is Rufus a group," began a *Rolling Stone* review of *Rufu-sized,* "or is it Chaka Khan with a backup band? That's a tough one."

Yeah, and stuff like that made it tougher and tougher to maintain group morale. Things had definitely gotten more tense with Rufus, thanks to all the attention I got. Plus, we bickered more and more over material, especially over my desire to do more jazz. Things went from bad to worse, when Richard went to check out what was up with "Better Days" during the making of *Ask Rufus.* Not only had Richard written "Better Days," but his father also played on that track. So naturally, Richard was curious about how it was going.

André was at the console when Richard entered the studio. While listening to the playback and the piano, Richard commented on how good things sounded. After a beat, he left the studio to hang out in the green room.

About five minutes later, André went down the hall into find him.

"Can I talk to you for a minute?"

"Sure."

For some reason they took their talk into a restroom that was about the size of a closet. Once there, André sounded off on Richard, with something to the effect of "Don't you ever tell me what to do!" The next thing Richard knew, André cold-cocked him.

André continued to pound Richard's head. The room was

so tight, Richard was helpless to avoid the blows. Andre, about six feet five inches, weighed roughly 350 pounds; Richard was about five feet nine inches and 140.

Richard's screams were so loud they registered on the monitor inside the studio. Long story short: when I got to the bathroom, I whacked André upside his head with a Courvoisier bottle (which didn't break as in the movies). And next, André was all over me. By then, a roadie and some of the guys in the band were on the scene, too.

That wasn't the first time the guys had to pull André off me. He had done so during our first run at Whisky A Go-Go when we were on the bill with zany Iggy Pop, notorious for peeing on the audience, breaking bottles on stage, and doing other really weird stuff.

At Whisky A Go-Go, Rufus would do a set, then Iggy, then Rufus, then Iggy. On one night, we were asked to do a double show, because Iggy had gone too far in his first set and cut himself pretty badly. I was game to do a double—as long as we got Iggy's money. André thought we should be grateful for the extra stage time with our without extra pay. When I stood my ground, André jumped all over me—pregnant with Milini. If the rest of the band hadn't been there to pull him off me . . . I don't want to think about what might have happened.

Richard wanted to sue André for attacking him, but our manager and the rest of the band members talked him out of it. We were about to release an album. A family feud would be bad publicity.

A few weeks later, our "happy family" was at the Grammys

with about a thousand people—the guys, the Bobs, agents, whoever—keeping distance between André and Richard. Richard's bandaged head was swollen to the size of a basketball and his eyes were black and blue.

André was soon out of Rufus. I had had it. I told the guys they had to choose: André or me. And I never spoke to André again. Sadly, when he later married Natalie, I sort of lost a friend. We would always be there for each other, and I never stopped loving her. But I couldn't be but so close to her, spend but so much time with her as long as she was with André.

Andre's ouster is how John Robinson came to be our drummer. Soon, we also had another keyboardist (and damned good songwriter) Dave Wolinski, aka "Hawk."

The new guys were cool. But needless to say, after the incident with André, I was having even *less* of a good time with Rufus.

Chaka was the start of my declaration of independence.

15

THE END OF A LOVE AFFAIR

I decamped to New York for the making of *Chaka,* because I'd signed on with Warner. That record company was on the case from the get-go. For one, they paired me up with a maestro of a producer and arranger, Arif Mardin. I knew what he had done for Bette Midler, Donny Hathaway, Roberta Flack, and Aretha, so you know I was jazzed about working with him.

I never imagined that Arif and I would work together for something like ten years, and that he and his wife, Latifah, would become like family. Plus, what with their being Turkish, they brought another world into my life.

The music world is littered with artists who stepped out of their pack to cut a solo, and then beat a hasty retreat back to their group, or slipped into oblivion because that first outing was a flop. I had moments of anxiety during the making of *Chaka,* but I never feared failure. In part, because I had Arif; in part because Warner was really together and totally behind me; in part because I focused on the music, not on "but what if . . ."

What an absolute relief it was to be out from under democracy! I was like a kid in a candy store since I had so much say on everything. Once the word got out that I was working on a solo album, we were flooded with demos. At night, often while taking one of my super baths by candlelight, I listened to demo after demo, usually knowing very early on whether I needed to listen long or—*Next!*

The other great thing about making *Chaka* was being able to have my brother on board.

Mark had been blessed with a perfect ear. Little Mr. Rhythm Mouth with his sounds as a kid. Mimicking came so easy. Other kids sometimes *paid* him to sing. Michael Jackson, James Brown, Al Green—just make a request. Mark could impersonate anyone.

Singing for friends was one thing. Anything beyond that— no way. He'd turn out for talent shows, just to watch, all the while thinking, "I could do that."

Mark was about fourteen when, during a visit home, I dropped a bass on him out of the blue. Next thing we knew, Mark was all-guitar all the time, and steady becoming his own best teacher—buying music books, checking out neighborhood bands, watching them rehearse, studying their moves, seeing where he could improve. At home, he'd hide in his room, practice for hours, usually backgrounded by some Earth, Wind, and Fire.

Once in L.A., Mark was something of a regular at Rufus rehearsals and those of whatever group Bonnie was with at the time. He also began to make his own way with local bands. By age nineteen, Mark was on the road with me, having put together a dynamite band for the *Chaka* tour. He would not only be my musical director, but also serve as something of a protector: trying to block people from giving me drugs, trying to fend off moochers, and grabbing me for hasty retreats whenever I had too much to drink—because I was prone to getting very nasty and telling people exactly what I thought.

"Regular" folks—"Hell, no, I don't remember your ass."

Celebrities too—"Bitch, I never did think you could sing."

Charming.

Before then, Mark and I had a blast working on *Chaka,* teaming up with his friend Keith Boyd, Jr. on "Some Love" and "We Got the Feeling" (with the bonus of George Benson).

When Arif told me Ashford and Simpson had written a song for me—hell yeah, I wanted to hear it. When I did, I knew instantly that "I'm Every Woman" was definitely for me.

That song was right on time. Disco ruled in '78—electro-disco, funk-disco, disco-disco—from Chic's "Le Freak," to Donna Summers' remake of "MacArthur Park," Gloria Gaynor's "I Will Survive," Rod Stewart's "Do Ya Think I'm Sexy," and Sylvestre's "You Make Me Feel (Mighty Real)." *Saturday Night Fever* was having quite the long life. And so would *Chaka.*

While I was doing *Chaka*, Rufus did the album *Numbers* without me, but we weren't through. There was the album that became *Street Player* to do, with "Stay," which was sort of ironic, what with all the buzz about would I or wouldn't I stay with Rufus.

As for Richard and I, we were on the edge of calling it quits, but then, I happened to get pregnant. We decided to stay together and hope for better days. As I'd done with Milini, the minute I found out I was pregnant, I sobered up and stayed clean throughout the pregnancy.

But I didn't stay happy. Richard and I were far from having better days: once I almost blasted him to smithereens.

I had been over at my mother's (where I'd been spending a lot of time those days). As I was about to head back to Laurel Canyon, I realized I didn't have my house keys. So I called Richard. Since he was on his way out, I asked him to leave the key for me in one of our secret key spots.

It was late at night when I reached home. I was tired, heavy (around eight months) and I had Milini in tow. No key.

I had to break a window to get into the house. Richard had just gone out drinking and forgotten all about me.

When he got back I lit into him quick.

I went off!

He went off!

We both went off!

At one point, all this going-off was happening in the kitchen, where I broke a dish, then he broke a dish, then I broke another dish, then he knocked a row of dishes off a shelf. And

I hit him. And he tagged me over the eye.

I went for the shotgun, loaded it, pulled the trigger.

I missed him because as soon as he saw the gun, he high-tailed it into the office, slammed the door, and turned out the lights.

I don't know if he was hiding in a closet or a corner, when I busted down the door and shot up the room. It's a miracle he didn't get hit.

When I came to my senses, as blood trickled from the wound above my eye, I wanted to damn myself to hell that Milini had witnessed something like this—not that it was the first fight she ever saw, but it was definitely the worst.

I called the cops and made like there was an intruder in the house.

"There's a man in my house and he's decked me over my eye, I'm pregnant, and you better come before I kill him or something!"

What happened between my call and the cops pinning Richard down and cuffing him is a blur. The last thing I remember as I headed out the house with Milini was the sight of Richard down on the floor trying to prove he lived there.

Amazingly, I felt steady enough to drive to my mother's, though having a police escort helped.

When the cops came, they escorted Milini and me to my mother's place.

So there I was, an almost felon, the mother of a six-year-old, and with another baby on the way, in a screwed up marriage, with bills on top of bills. And there were thousands of women out there envying Chaka Khan, thinking if only they were me . . .

Another C-section. Because I could choose the day of delivery, at first I thought, my birthday! Then I wondered whether that wouldn't just fuel some sibling rivalry. I chose the day before my birthday instead and chose my hospital room, too: one with a view.

I had wanted a boy, and on March 22, 1979, my wish came true: Damien, we named him. After that demon child from *Omen?* people always ask. No! We loved the spirit of Hesse's *Max Demian* (Richard decided on the alternate spelling). For a middle name, I chose Patrick, after my maternal grandfather.

While I knew people around me worried about how difficult life can be in America for a bi-racial child, Richard and I hadn't focused on it. We didn't choose his identity, but decided to let that be his choice. As it turned out, he didn't have some heavy decision to make because, yes, he came out light, but not light enough to pass for white. Too, when he got older he claimed black.

For help with the new baby, I asked Gramma Maude to pack her bags and come live with us in Calabasas (though I knew my days up there were numbered).

It wasn't all that long after Damien was born that I was back in the studio for *Masterjam* with Rufus. MCA, which had gobbled up ABC by then, was hell-bent on us having a smash. Enter Q.

He had recently wrapped on George Benson's *Give Me the Night* and the gloved one's *Off the Wall*. Who wouldn't think Quincy Jones and Rufus a great match? He and I had hit with "Stuff Like That" for his *Sounds . . . And Stuff Like That!* Bobby, Hawk, and John had worked on *Off the Wall*.

Masterjam will have its magic, go platinum, but no one will think it's a masterpiece. A little schizophrenic, some say: as in not-very-Rufus and too-much-Quincy. For me, it was just the fulfillment of a contractual obligation and an opportunity to work with Quincy again who, like Arif, became like an uncle to me. But I sure wasn't loving what I was feeling with Rufus, or with the rest of my life.

It was around the time of the release of *Masterjam*'s chief hit, "Do You Love What You Feel," that David Nathan conducted what he termed "the strangest interview" he ever did with us.

We met at a hotel in Manhattan, and initially it was just me, Kevin Murphy, Tony Maiden, Bobby Watson, and David Wolinski. Sometime in the middle of the interview session, Chaka stumbled in and acted very strange. She kept pacing back and forth, staring out the window, and literally speaking over band members as I asked questions. It was obvious from the expression on the faces of Murphy and Wolinski in particular that all wasn't well in the camp.

I tuned in, I zoned out. At one point, I barged in with: "I think art is pure, and I think it's been raped and whored be-

141

cause of greed and selfishness—people no longer respect music as an art form the way they should. And that, to me, is a real sin."

Obviously, bringing another life into the world had not inspired me to stay clean. And Richard and I were not having better days on Magic Mountain. Plus, I swear that house was haunted.

I'd never felt we were alone in that house. Friends claimed to have experienced some pretty weird stuff in the guest room—(and, no, they weren't high). Then, for a stretch, every night, a bit past eleven—THUD . . . THUD . . . THUD—hard, heavy, deliberate stomps on the roof, back and forth, from one end to the other, back and forth—THUD . . . THUD . . .

One night, the stomps sifted into my sleep, along with a Native American dude, in silhouette, with a bullhorn hat. He was walking back and forth on the roof—THUD . . . THUD . . . THUD. He had a cobalt blue lantern in his hands. THUD, THUD, THUD.

I told Gramma Maude about my dream the next morning. She was neither perplexed nor perturbed.

"Look," she said, "we live on this planet with all manner of life. You cannot buy into the fear. Once you get some understanding . . . come to grips with the fact that we are not here alone . . ." Gramma Maude's prescription? "Relax."

As soon as I cooled out about the THUD, THUD, THUD, it stopped.

But then, two of our dogs inexplicably died. And one morning, when I went into the garage reserved for the rabbits,

I found the cages strewn all about. I saw blood and scattered rabbit fur. What in the—but the garage had been locked. The rabbit cages suspended, *securely*, from a beam. What—how— could anything get to them? A godzilla (and acrobatic) rat?

Back behind the house, was a cave in which Richard had found arrowheads. The place was also known as Las Virginas, because, according to legend, fourteen Native American virgins had been slaughtered there in some long ago era. But I only found this out after the fact! Had I known before, there's no way in hell I would have agreed to move into that house, which Richard ended up with (mortgaged to the hilt) when our divorce came through in '80.

And I didn't stop to mourn the end of what once had been such a wonderful love affair for even a moment. Now I know what a mistake that was, but back then I was sticking with my M.O.: *Next!* Better to just focus on career.

Rufus's (without me) *Party Til You're Broke,* came out around the time of my *Naughty,* with Nick and Val's "Clouds," on which a young singer with much promise sang background: Whitney Houston. Also on *Naughty* was Luther Vandross' "Papillon," (aka "Hot Butterfly") and a bunch of other songs I really dug. *Next!*

On *What Cha' Gonna Do For Me* I really got to mix it up, from the kicky title song to riffing on "A Night in Tunisia" with Dizzy doing a solo along with Bird (via "cut and paste" of course) to getting a bit Brazilian with "I Know You, I Live You." *Next!*

I wasn't even in the studio with Rufus for *Camouflage,*

which one reviewer summed up as "dreck." *Next!*

Rufus moved to Warner, where an A&R guy came up with the concept for the band's farewell: a double-album rooted in three-nights of greatest hits at New York's Savoy Ballroom in the winter of '82. We'd top it off with four new songs, one of which will be one of my forever favorites, Hawk's "Ain't Nobody," a song that has it all—a bad beat, cute words, fabulous melody—one of the few songs I never tire of singing.

Next on the solo front, *Chaka Khan*—not a megaseller but out of it came two Grammys: Best R& B Female Performance and, in a way, even sweeter, Best Vocal Arrangement (with Arif) for the "Be-Bop Medley." For the next album, I did something pretty different with Stanley Clarke, Chick Corea, Joe Henderson, Freddie Hubbard, and Lenny White, when I went all the way jazz with *Echoes of an Era.*

Soon after the release of *Live: Stompin' at the Savoy,* in August '83, it was official: Chaka was solely solo.

16

PAPILLON

"ChakaChakaChaka—Cha-ka Khan, Cha-ka Khan . . ."

In '84, Prince had his *Purple Rain;* Tina, *Private Dancer;* Oprah, her own show, and a lot of folks had been fretting about "What does Jesse want?" When "I Feel for You" hit the street I was in the news too.

I had thought about doing "I Feel for You" ever since Prince released it on his second album in '79. By then, Prince and I had already gotten to know each other—though the first time I laid eyes on him I wanted to smack him.

I met Prince because he tricked me, some time in the '70s, while I was doing a gig in San Francisco.

I was in a hotel room when my phone rang.

"I didn't know you were in town!" It had been a long time

since I'd seen or spoken to Sly (yes, of the Family Stone).

Could I come meet him at the studio he was working in?

"Sure!"

I'd been chilling with a friend, who came along for the drive. When we got to the studio, we couldn't find Sly, or anybody else for that matter, until we stepped into this one little room and spied this skinny little guy with a humungous Afro.

"You seen Sly?"

"That was me that called you."

"And who the hell are you?"

Even back then, Prince was so very seductive. As we started talking about I don't remember what, I wasn't able to stay pissed at Prince for long. I found myself wishing him well on the album he was working on. That was the beginning of our friendship. Not that we got close right away, but we kept in touch.

Some time later, I was with a friend who was playing Prince's album. One song caught me. "Ooh, that's a great song!"

"Yeah, great song, alright," my friend replied. He thought the whole album was great. "But, it's over now," he added.

"Aw, that's a shame." "I Feel for You" stayed a "friend of mind."

Echoes of an Era had not been financially successful and Warner was pressing for something very pop, very commercial. So when I got to work on the next album—*Now, I'll do that*

Prince song. I figured "I Feel for You" would satisfy Warner, for starters.

Not long after I laid down my tracks on that song, I got a call from Arif.

"You must come in, my dear, and hear what I've done."

When I stepped into the studio, that was the first time I heard "ChakaChakaChaka—Cha-ka Khan, Cha-ka Khan . . ."

"That is so whack!"

"Don't worry, my dear," Arif tried to calm me down. "It will be a hit."

I guess we can call him Arif "Amazing Kreskin" Mardin.

Arif had arranged it all, from Grandmaster Melle Mel's rap to Stevie's harmonica solo.

No one was as surprised as I at the way that song blew up and that it was nominated for a Grammy.

I had been so sure Tina would get Best R&B Female Vocal, I hadn't even prepared any remarks. I was there waiting to cheer for Tina, when the winner was—

"Chaka Khan for 'I Feel for You.'"

I don't even remember getting up on stage, but a whole lot of folks remembered what I said.

"Thank you."

That was it. "Thank you" and Cha-ka Khan Cha-ka Khan was outta there.

A bunch of people felt dissed. They saw my simple "thank you" as a serious dereliction of duty to acknowledge all their help on the album or their love and support over the years.

As I told *Blues & Soul,* "I think that's all bull anyway—I

mean after a while you get sick and tired of hearing everyone tell you how much they wanted to thank this one that one—everyone!—from the mailroom clerk to their great-grand-mother!"

That's how I felt. Plus, while I certainly appreciate awards—and this was my fifth Grammy—I've never gotten a big high from winning awards. For one thing, I know they have been the ruination of many careers. Awards can make an artist lazy. I think my tendency to shove awards in a closet or under a bed is part of my strategy for not letting awards go to my head.

With the "I Feel for You" Grammy, another piece of my quick "Thank you" was the issue of detachment. I felt really distanced from that album. The pressure had been so intense to have a *commercial* album, I let myself get a bit "bullied" into having not a lot of say. I'm not looking a gift horse in the mouth. *I Feel for You* went platinum; that album did a lot for me careerwise. But "I Feel for You" was far from my favorite song. Neither were the other songs that hit: "This is Your Night" and "Through the Fire" (a truly great song but not a favorite).

My favorite song on that album is "Caught in the Act." I never get many requests for that, but just let me do a concert and leave "I Feel for You" out—I'm likely to be tarred and feathered! *This* is the ball and chain.

And thanks to that song I have guys forever coming up to me telling me they want "to rock" me.

Puh-leeze—don't tell me what you feel for me!

At times, I've wanted to ask a guy, *How would you feel if*

some guy ran up on your wife, your girl, your mother with that shit? Poetic justice some say, given my public persona. I am ever grateful to Isabel Wilkerson for the line she wrote in a feature on me for *Essence*: "A few things to know about Chaka Khan. First, DO NOT COME UP TO HER AND CHANT IN HER EAR "CHA-KA KHAN, CHA-KA KHAN," AS IF YOU ARE MELLE MEL OR SOMETHING. (emphasis added!) Thank you, Isabel for getting the word out!

When "I Feel For You" hit Cha-ka Khan, Cha-ka Khan was living in the Big Apple. Had been for a while. I was sick of moderate weather all year round. I wanted some drastic seasonal changes—they keep you on your toes in a way.

In a place like New York, it takes a different kind of energy to take care of yourself in the summer than it does in winter. In a place like New York, you get to live the death-rebirth cycle of life because you live with nature doing just that in a striking way, as the winter with its (for the most part) naked trees and brown ground, gives way to mad March (and you never know what you'll get in that month). Then, the April showers and then life!—and color, color, color—up from the ground, up on the trees. You get to be lazy and lush summer (and craving for cool when the dog days hit!) When autumn rolls around, the changing leaves and the nip in the breeze—your spirit gets crisp. Then it's back to the hibernating vibe of a winter with its cold, its sometimes snow, its darkness so early.

Too, if truth be told, I was feeling my mother was meddling in my life way too much—telling me how to live my life, how to raise my children. So I packed my bags once again and kicked it the Big Apple, bringing Milini and Damien with me.

And I was in love with Albee. Had been for a while.

Albee and I had met through a friend back in the late '70s when I was in New York to make my first solo album. On the surface, we didn't have a lot in common. He was Jewish and I was *still* black and religiously uncommitted. I was a singer; he taught in a public school in Harlem. SO what was the attraction? It was more than our mutual affection for getting plenty high. Albee wasn't teaching for a paycheck. He really cared about children and I really admired that about him.

"We are really perfectly matched," I told a writer for *Rolling Stone*. I commented on the obvious—"his salary is no where near mine," and then pointed out that "he still brings his money in. He didn't give up his job like my two . . . husbands did—immediately stop work and groove and say, 'My work is now you.' That is a bunch of bullshit. No woman wants to hear that. A woman wants to wake up in the morning to the smell of aftershave lotion and not see anybody there." (Perfectly matched? Surprise, surprise, Albee and I won't be an everlasting love.)

I had time for this interview because mid-tour my voice went out and I had no choice but to take a week off. That's why I was home letting this journalist check out my life.

The furnishings are comfortable, not elegant, like the puffy blue sofas in the living room, where photos of Chaka dominate the walls. At two in the afternoon, she is still wearing a robe and mukluks while watching TV from atop her Paul Bunyan-size bed. She has set aside a copy of *The National Lampoon* in favor of a horror movie called *Salem's Lot*. On the bookshelves are a slew of sci-fi and horror best sellers, with titles like *Monster, Inferno, Dread Companion.* "Stephen King is my favorite author," Chaka says. "And I like all the horror movies. They do scare me. Some people say that fear is sexual. I don't know if that's true. I just like to scare myself."

The writer noted that eleven-year-old Milini had picture after picture of Prince all over her room, and that when five-year-old son Damien came home from school, the first thing he did was play *Purple Rain*. We certainly were one Prince-loving family!

This writer had started the article with a snapshot of me on the town.

The sky is filled with dark thunderclouds, a chilly wind is sweeping the first drops of rain against the windows of Atlanta, and Chaka Khan is going to a gay bar to watch female impersonators. Earlier, she had swooped into the Rib Room, The Tower Place Hotel's all-but-deserted restaurant, in a strapless red dress with a skirt the size of a patio umbrella. After a few Heinekens and a bottle of champagne to enliven this lonely night off, she wandered into the gift shop and bought sweat shirts and junk jewelry.

It wasn't long before she was trundling off with the cashier and a group of his male friends to the bar, Illusions, to hear a man in a stunning dress sing her hit single. Chaka herself got up and knocked off the second half of "I Feel for You," wailing it into every corner of the bar. And then, around six in the morning, she headed home clutching a memento from the cashier, a sack holding a loaf of homemade pumpkin bread.

I'm sure I was grateful but I had no particular passion for pumpkin bread. When people ask about my favorite things, they are often surprised that the list is neither very long nor very grand.

I love frankincense and myrrh incense, bath stuff, scented candles, the smell of pine, TV, books, my couch and blanky. I've never been into jewelry, really (especially really expensive jewelry). If anything, I like a little gold sometimes and semi-precious stones—tiger eye, amber, amethyst, garnet, malachite—any of those colors that take me to Ancient.

I also like my herbs. (And, no, weed wasn't my only herb.) Thanks to the brothers and sisters at Affro-Arts, I started learning at an early age about the rejuvenating and healing possibilities of herbs. One of the pleasures of life when I'm not on the road has always been to be able to cook with an array of quality herbs. I love them all—rosemary, oregano, basil, cilantro—and don't forget the hot peppers! My mother says I put garlic on everything. Well, almost on everything. And one of the wonderful things about New York is that you can find any herb, any seasoning, and all kinds of foods from every culture in the world.

After spending so much time in the land of the laid-backs, the Big Apple forced me to pick up my pace. It was that, or get trampled. People moving fast, fast, fast, morning, noon, night, past midnight, in this 24-hour city, where you can find anything your heart desires. And I got caught up in dangerous desires. In New York, you can also party till you drop. Boy, did I party! And, boy, did I drop!—trying to forget my pain, trying to drown memories of a younger Milini climbing into my suitcase when I was heading out for the road; trying not to think about what it might be like for Milini and Damien to not have full-time fathering but always having a transient, not very responsible mother, who embarrassed them with the outfits she wore on the rare occasion that she made a visit to their schools. And while I dropped and dropped and dropped—I was on my way to cop when I got hit by a truck.

I was at an intersection on the Upper West Side. I don't think the truck even tried to slow down, let alone stop. It was a full-on broadside.

My Bronco flipped over once, twice, slid a ways down the street.

"You . . . alright?" My brother was in the car with me.

"Yeah . . . You alright?"

Mark had not one injury. Other than feeling knocked into the next day, along with the disorientation that comes with finding yourself upside down, my only injury was a cut on my lip. A photo of me with a Good Samaritan's handkerchief pressed against my mouth made it into *Jet*, along with the claim that I was crying. I was not! I was rejoicing that I wasn't mangled or dead. (And I'm not trying to drop a PSA in here, but just so you know, we were wearing our seat belts.)

In a way, a cut lip wasn't the only damage. The accident happened not too long before I was scheduled to do a Diet Coke commercial. The stitches wouldn't permit me to do the commercial, and Diet Coke wasn't able to wait for my lip to heal up. So Whitney ended up singing "Just for the Taste of It" instead of me. Some family members and friends were really bummed about my losing that commercial (and the mega bucks it paid). Not me. The fact that I'd survived the accident without monster damage was uppermost in my mind.

And during my Big Apple days of dropping and copping and getting hit by a truck, I also drummed.

I've often thought I might have become a drummer if I didn't have a voice. I started playing around with the drums during my late teens. Like singing, never taking formal lessons, just picking it up.

Over the years, I've jammed on the drums with friends in my house, in their homes, in after-hours joints in whatever city I'm in, including when I lived in New York. But only when I was emboldened by booze (Cape Codders my first choice). Unless I was drunk, I didn't have the nerve to take to the drums because I wasn't that secure in my skills.

While living a dizzying pace in New York, there were lots of gigs and the making of more albums—*Destiny* and *Perfect Fit* both out in '86. *Patchwork*, '87; and then in '88, *CK*.

CK never came close to being my best album, but it will always be the one with a very special place in my heart. This is, in part, because on it I did "I'll Be Around" and "The End of a Love Affair," two songs I heard so often as a child—every time Gramma Maude played her *Lady in Satin* album.

The big thing, for me , about *CK*—bigger than Billie Holiday—was Miles.

My father worshipped Miles. When I was a child, he had me convinced that in the pantheon of jazz greats, Miles Davis was El Supremo. When I got older, that conviction became totally my own.

I loved Miles's spirit as much as I loved his music. How could I not connect with his maverick, renegade ways? What guts it took for this scion of the black bourgeoisie to chuck his parents' expectations and walk his own path.

His cockiness never bothered me. I know some people got mad at Miles for sometimes performing with his back to the audience, but I understood where he was coming from.

He was like, *it's my horn! Listen to the trumpet! This is AUDIO—Listen!*

That's what jazz, the thinking person's music, is all about, *listening.* You don't need pyrotechnics, you don't need razzle-dazzle. Nothing should distract from the sound. *Listen!* It's not about the artist, it's all about the music. *Listen!* Working with Miles was a dream come true.

We met not long after I moved to New York, thanks to my friend Charlotte, who used to do background for Bette Midler.

"You want to go to Miles' party?" Charlotte asked one day.

"Are you fucking kidding? Hell, yeah."

I don't remember the occasion, only that it was a garden party at Miles's place on the Upper West Side, one of those stone really Medieval looking townhouses—gorgeous.

As soon as Miles saw me, he ran over to me, got on his knees, stuck his head in my crotch. Trust me, I beat him back quick. I was not having that!

And that was the beginning of our friendship, our hanging out together at Mikells, the Brecker Brothers' Seventh Avenue South, and other clubs, listening, listening, listening to jazz. Our friendship led to my being, as far as I know, the only vocalist he ever performed with. We jammed at clubs and a couple of times at the Montreux Jazz Festival, most memorably the one in the summer of '89, preserved on *Miles in Montreux,* with my rendition of Michael Jackson's "Human Nature."

In a way, I have Miles to thank for not losing my voice.

As any singer—or anyone who does a lot of public speaking—will tell you, it's no biggie to lose your voice, an occasional bout of laryngitis comes with the territory.

There came a point where I had no high ends, and no low notes. I had to sing mid-range and it was killing me.

"Polyps" said New York's top throat doctor. I didn't freak because I knew singers get polyps (especially opera and rock singers). And I had been singing strong for many years, doing a lot of yelling and screaming (on and off stage), and smoking, drinking, drugging, and partying till I dropped.

The surgery would be a snap, the doctor assured me, and I had no doubts, no fears. The hard part—the scary part—came after the surgery: I had to shut up for two weeks—complete silence. Not one whisper. Not a chuckle. Not nothing. That meant isolation.

My manager at the time had a friend who was out of town, and willing to let me crash at this place in Greenwich Village. (My housekeeper/nanny would stay with Milini and Damien.)

Even with the isolation from family and friends, I wasn't sure I'd be able to shut up. Two whole weeks of talking via a chalkboard! Man, I didn't think I could make it. Then I thought of Miles.

Miles had had the same surgery, and in the midst of his shut-up time, something was going on with the promoter that he wasn't happy with, and his trademark temper got the best of him. And he yelled. And that was the wreck of his voice. Miles once had a beautiful voice, could have been one hell of a singer.

So whenever I felt the temptation to talk all I had to do was think of Miles. In fact, at the top my chalkboard I wrote, "Miles Davis."

Miles gave me the biggest compliment I've ever gotten from a musician—"You sing like my horn."

He thrillingly confirmed something I'd long felt: that I was never really singing, but playing my voice, which I saw as a horn, an alto sax.

Miles and Prince were tight, too. I don't recall where we were, but one night we three started talking about doing a CD together. I was getting ready to work on *CK*, so I thought, until Miles, Prince and I could do our masterjam—

"Miles, come on in on this CD."

"Why don't we all do a track?" said Prince.

"Cool!"

That was the genesis of Prince's "Sticky Wicked."

That was the only song Miles was supposed to be on. But one day in the studio, he was like, "What's next?"

And I was like, "Put on some tape Arif, and let him play." And that's how he ended up on "I'll be Around." A few years later, Miles wasn't. And we'd never gotten around to making that album together.

When I heard of his death, I didn't freak. I'd been ready. I'd seen him not too long before he passed.

We were both in Amsterdam, doing the jazz festival in The Hague, staying at the same hotel. I was just coming into the hotel, when his people met up with me in the lobby.

"Chaka, glad you're here. Miles is really sick. He's asking for you."

I went right up to his room.

He had arthritis, high blood pressure, everything—his joints were so stiff; he couldn't do shit. I had his people go get some camphor, some eucalyptus oil, and any muscle relaxation bath mix they could find (and Europe is really good for that stuff). They came back with oodles of stuff.

I had Miles take a bath, a long soak, with his arms totally submerged, the water up to his neck. I believe I also had him take some aloe vera and some type of herbal tea, chamomile perhaps. I made him just rest, and it helped. But I knew he would not be with us much longer. He knew, too. So, as I said, when he died months after that, I was ready. By then, I was based in England, where I had beat a hasty retreat to save my life.

But back before the move to England, back before the magic of singing with Miles in Montreux and on *CK,* came the day I had to go to my father's rescue.

17

LOVE ME STILL

If you asked my father when it all started, he'd probably say, "When I was born."

He had been a preemie, coming into the world at about two pounds. His first crib was a dresser drawer in a rooming house. That he lived at all was something of a miracle. He was his father's first son, and he would one day reflect on what a trauma his birth must have been for his father, how disappointed he must have been to get this puny little baby, instead of a big strapping boy.

My father never did grow up to be a big and strong boy. Years and years later, when my father was living in Hollywood, clerking at a brokerage house, he started having problems with his legs. Poor circulation. Pain.

He compensated with a lot of aspirin. Ditto when he moved to Berkeley, with a sore on his right foot that just wouldn't heal. By the time he got himself to a hospital things were out of control.

"Yvette, you gotta come get me. I'm lying here in this room . . . with my foot cut off and . . . my mother and all these people I don't know are standing in the doorway." I freaked the fuck out.

By then, I had skipped out of New York, and was back in California, living in Beverly Hills. A friend was at my place when my father called. He helped me get something like calm, and was at the ready to help me help my father. We got the first flight out we could.

Here is my hand for you to hold
Here's the part of me they have not sold
I've wandered far, I've had my fill
I need you now, do you love me still

I found my father, hollowed-eyed and skinny, in a dinky, dingy, dirty, nasty-ass rented room, where he'd been alone for about ten days, doing a pitiful job of feeding himself, and dressing his wound. He and Connie had been divorced for a while by then. He was alone.

You could see the bone. His foot looked like a dog had bitten it, gnawed it off, from the instep down to the toes.

I wanted to sue the hell out of that hospital: you are not supposed to send an amputee home until a wound is closed and healed! The hospital, one of Oakland's worst, had sent my father home too soon after the surgery, with a bag full of bandages and not enough pain pills.

For the first time in my life, I saw my father cry. He was crying and crying and I wanted to blot that moment out of my mind. I couldn't stop crying either. Children are not supposed to see their parents pathetic. Parents are supposed to be forever the caretakers, we all want to believe even though we've lived through other elders growing old, getting sick, going to a hospital and never coming back. But we don't want to face the fact that one day we will have to deal with the details of our parents' ailments, their decline.

I gave him some pain pills I'd brought with me (leftovers from some dental work). I got him something like washed up, dressed. My friend put him on his back. We cabbed it to the airport.

In L.A., I got my father into an excellent hospital near Beverly Hills. I had a live Christmas tree—all decked out—delivered to his private room. I put plenty of presents beneath it.

The hospital got him to better health, but there was no saving his leg.

When he was released, I moved him into my suite at the Beverly Hills Hotel: my interim, until I could move into a nearby condo I'd decided on.

I got my father a nurse and every comfort. When I was working, I kept in touch, called often.

So many smiles and lies surround me

Empty expectations, faceless fears
Sometimes this life is a bitter pill
I love you now, do you love me still

When I moved into my new place, I moved my father in with me. He loved living rich. When I was home, we got high, talked shit, cooked our favorite foods, played music, got high, made like we hadn't a care in the world: as if my mother hadn't declared me too messed up to be a mother and taken Milini and Damien to live with her.

"The kids are so worried about you! How could you do this to them? They know what you're doing."

"Yeah, Mama, I know they know what I'm doing because I told them what I'm doing." At the time, I thought I deserved a medal for not getting high right in front of their face.

"You had a mother who was always there for you. Your children deserve better than this."

And by then, I had hooked up with a man who was an asshole, living off me, living with me. Also staying with me were Bonnie and a girlfriend of mine who had gotten in a jam and had no place for her and her little boy to crash.

I couldn't stay with my father for the whole of his convalescence. I couldn't blow off a three-month European tour, couldn't risk getting sued or getting the rep as a no-show, couldn't forfeit a payday to pay for the penthouse and all its trappings, the drugs, my food, other people's food, the makeup, the hair, the people on the payroll, the show-time clothes, the clothes friends take a liking to and never return, my father's care. Then again, Europe has always been my breath of fresh air.

Not long after I returned from Europe, my father, by then fitted with his prosthetic, went to Chicago to visit his mother who was ailing. After about six months in Chicago, Daddy returned to Berkeley, where in a few years time, he developed a stubborn sore on his left foot and lost his left leg. And I bought him a top-of-the-line wheelchair—whatever he wanted—and decided I'd take care of him for the rest of his life.

That I bear my father no ill will for being a poor parent will always gall some people. I usually take Billie Holiday's advice, "Don't Explain." What can you say to people who don't understand the power of forgiveness, of letting things go, making the best of what you've got—you know, a glass-half-full take on life.

He may not have been a good father by other people's definition (or mine). But I believe you have to take people for who they are and not try to make them who you want them to be. So he wasn't a perfect father, but he was a friend, a mentor of sorts. He gave me what he could—a love for travel, for learning, for not living lock-step with the norm, thinking beyond the status quo. And he gave me music.

To a certain extent, I am my father. To hate him would be to hate myself.

With my father, I never felt I had to stifle myself. Our relationship was the closest thing I'd ever known to unconditional love. No matter the crazy, insane, and wrong things I did, he was one of the few people in my family who never judged me (I guess you could say he had a people-who-live-in-glass-houses approach to life.) And for that, I am eternally grateful. As I am for a bit of advice he gave me years ago.

We were in L.A. It was night. We were outside Whisky A Go-Go looking up at my name on the marquee.

"Yvette, always remain humble," he said. "Stay humble."

I took his advice to heart. Heeding it has at times been a struggle. Stardom can definitely get you tripping. On occasion, I've gone a bit diva on people—gotten in a "peel-me-a grape" mode. One of the biggest traps of fame is you get used to a lot of people doing a lot of things for you. And this can infantilize you, make it hard for you to stay in touch.

Stay humble.

Whenever I've gotten pseudo diva with someone, I've always kicked myself afterwards, reminded myself that if I get cut I bleed red blood just like everyone else. But I don't beat up on myself too much because, after all, I know there are a whole lot of people, from teachers to cashiers to sanitation workers, who get diva on people and who have gone off on total strangers. One of the times I did that I was en route to somewhere, in a layover in Jamaica.

I noticed this guy eyeing me, noticed his camera too. When he headed in our direction, I took a deep breath and tried to get patient.

He asked if he could take a picture.

"Not now okay, give me a minute." I don't remember what my crew and I were into, but it was not a good time for a Kodak moment.

He walked away as if he was going to be patient but then looped back around and soon, he was snapping, snapping, snapping.

"I TOLD YOU NOT NOW MOTHERFUCKER! WHY THE FUCK COULDN'T YOU WAIT A DAMN FUCKING MINUTE!"

Charming.

Okay, it would have been better had I not cussed him out. But was that being diva? How would you feel if a stranger started taking pictures of you without your permission?

Strangers can sometimes strain the desire to be "regular." That syrupy adoration that comes over some people creates a chasm. Instead of my being able to carry on a conversation with a "regular person" I meet, they've got stardust in their eyes, and they're all nervous, which puts me on edge. But I can't complain really; when I signed on for this business, I signed on for a whole lot of stuff like that (like having to change my phone number a few times a year). And my father had told me it would, at times, be hard to maintain.

Stay humble.

One of the ways I work at it is by not getting caught up in a whole lot of entourage. Unless it's a photo shoot, or a show that's being videotaped, I do my own hair and makeup for most performances. (And I'm no longer into flamboyant stage clothes, or drastic wardrobe changes between sets). When I'm on the road, I work at keeping it simple, and not amplifying my needs just because I'm a "star." For example, when I'm in a hotel, my biggest "demand" is for fresh pillows. And whatever bit of staff I have with me know that if I have an adequate supply of Perrier and cranberry juice I'm a happy camper.

Stay humble.

The night my father and I stood outside Whisky A Go-Go, I also wanted to remain a "regular" person, wanted to take pains to remain humble. My father's words gave me something to hold onto, made staying humble all the more something for me to strive for. I never stopped trying to please him.

> *You have been mine since time untold*
> *Our love is immortal, don't you know*
> *Others will come, and they will go*
> *But I loved you young, I love you old.*

And I'd never stopped loving him.

18

WHAT AM I MISSING?

When it came to loving myself that was a whole other matter. I kept living fast throughout the '80s, hurting myself with my lifestyle, receiving angry letters from my mother, calls from Tammy, pleading letters from Milini, begging me to stop my madness. But nobody could get me to stop living the high life. Or from moving again. Back to New York where I stayed out of control and where I one day left my penthouse on the Upper West Side and found myself out of my mind. It was '89 and the Berlin Wall wasn't the only thing that would fall.

As I left the building—*Bam!* It was as if the whole city smacked me in the face. The noise, the people-people-people, the light, the busy-busy, the light, that crazy New York energy, the light. I couldn't go on. I literally could not walk forward. I made an about-face, got my ass back up into my home in the sky where I stayed for days, days, days. Heroin was the only thing I could go on with.

Get out! You gotta get out!

That's the only clue I had. Something kept telling me, *Get Out!*

Another miracle. I was able to snatch myself away, and get it together enough to get out—out of the heroin, my apartment, New York, the country.

19

STRANGER TO LOVE

I had always felt so comfortable in Europe, especially in England, where I had a huge following. And they'd just gone mad over the remix album of my shake-your-booty hits, *Life Is a Dance*. So Londoners saw me, knew me, and were, for the most part, pretty cool. Sure, a bobby, shopkeeper, or lorry driver might say, "Hi," smile, wave, ask easy for an autograph; nobody got all stupid and in a frenzy. I was able to go about my business in peace—whether to pick up some herbs and garlic or a box of sanitary napkins—without finding myself at the head of a parade. Made a girl feel respected, appreciated for her talent versus being merely a fixation for stargazers.

I lived in a hotel for a while until I found a little apartment in Chelsea. Except for an occasional gig in Europe or the States, for about a year I did a whole lot of only whatever I wanted to do or not do. And in a way that was my most intense through-the-fire time because for the first time in my life I was alone. And that was a challenge.

I rested. I filled up on mysteries. I filled up on TV. "Ugly Americans" could snicker all they wanted about England only having a handful of channels, but what they broadcast was such a feast for the mind, as opposed to all that mind-numbing U.S. prime-time drivel.

I ranted a lot about the States those days, even to the press, because I didn't care who knew I was pissed. About the public school system going to the dogs, about the river of guns, and people who painted as crazies those who dared to suggest the drug flood was a conspiracy against the black community.

And what are you contributing?

I was angry that so many people kept blaming Africans for AIDS! And that the ranks of the working poor was swelling, while in practically every industry, from health care to prisons to toilet paper, the Powers-That-Be had adopted Gordon Gecko's credo: "Greed is good." My industry was certainly no exception.

"Commercial," Commercial" "Commercial!" Pap sells, make pap. Most radio stations were perfecting the art of re-dundancy, playing the s-o-s all the time. Where was the vision, the thirst for innovation, the balls to make the public stretch? But if the public seemed happy with pap in books, in movies, in music—Pap sells! Make pap!

It wasn't all bad, of course. There were groups and soloists out there doing more than just entertaining. And, of course I applauded in '91, when Pretty in Pink, the group my daughter formed at age fourteen, had their hit single and music video "It's All About You." All to end too soon when the record label, Motown, was hit with an injunction due to a legal dispute between two of the writers. And not only that: Milini got pregnant not long after the album was released.

Milini told me the news when I was in California for a visit. I was not happy. She wasn't yet twenty. I feared her marriage to the baby's father would be a disaster. If feared Milini was going to ruin her life. I pleaded with her to go to a counselor. Of course, there are always two sides to every story. To hear Milini tell it, I was *furious*—and encouraged her to have an abortion.

In the end, Milini did what she wanted to do. And once I got used to the idea that she was going to have a baby, I couldn't wait. (You know me: I love babies!)

"How does it feel to be a grandmother?" I never understood why some people tried to make it an issue, as if being a grandmother was some kind of negative mojo, something that started to make you prune up. I was going to be however old I was whether I was a grandmother or not.

By the time my grandbaby, Raeven Alexis Geanine was born, on May 28, '92, I was unsequestered. I had begun to move to strength when I started working on *The Woman I Am,* officially producing myself for the first time. Actually, I had always done that to varying degrees when it came to my vocal performance. *The Woman I Am* was the first time I got and took that credit.

173

I was pleased, very pleased with the product I put out. Others let me know they were pleased too by granting the album a Grammy. Chaka to Warner! Calling on Warner! Warner come the fuck in!" By and large, the public was clueless about *The Woman I Am*. Warner did diddly on the promo end.

Not only that. While I was touring to promote this album, my manager at the time, Steve Margo, met me out on the road to let me know that he'd been offered a job at Warner Brothers and was taking it. Lose some, win some.

Simone Morrison goes in the "win" category.

"You want the job. You got it." That was within five minutes of meeting Simone, who came to see me in '90 about the slot as my personal assistant. She had worked for the singer Karen Wheeler and had been recommended by Claudia Fontaine, one of my backup singers at the time. I didn't need to go through any long interview process. As soon as I met Simone, I could tell the spirit of this Rastawoman moved well with mine. Soon, Simone was wearing many hats. Eventually, she became my road manager.

By then, Simone had seen me through a lot of adventures. Such as the time I was in Venice to perform for Liz Taylor's charity event for AIDS. Simone and I were out shopping, sipping wine, strolling, checking out the cuties, sipping wine, when we came upon this beautiful church. I might leave home without AMEX, but never without a camera, and I just *had* to have a shot of this church across the canal from us.

As I made my way down the steps—I didn't see the moss. The next thing I knew all of me was in that nasty, stinking, murky water. I came up looking like a sewer rat, legs all scratched up, but other than that no major damage. (Audrey Hepburn had fallen into that same canal in the '50s—so at least I was in good company; unfortunately she had ended up with a recurring eye infection.)

The tabloids feasted on my mishap. For a while the whole town was talking about "Did you hear Chaka Khan fell into the canal?"

Being based in London meant being closer to Germany, where Harold lived. He was the host of a cultural arts show, TV and film producer, professor of philosophy, and author of many books—smart guy.

We had met in the mid-'80s, during one of my European tours. We had clicked and I'd given him my number. He called. We talked. (Albee sometimes had nice chats with him before handing me the phone.)

Once we were on the same continent, we talked a lot more, and there I was—in love again.

As I said, Harold was smart. We had long talks about philosophy, history, and poems of Rilke. During our talks and travels all around Europe, I learned more about opera, European history, European classical music, European food. Of course, he reminded me of my father.

For love of Harold, I took a place in Mannheim, and lived bicity, learning German in the process because I got tired of being clueless, particularly when I was out with Harold and one or more of his friends.

They always spoke English out of politeness. But let the meal go long, let the wine keep flowing and is it any wonder they soon lapsed into their mother tongue and I didn't know what or who in the hell they were talking about. So I made up my mind it was time for me to sprechen some Deutsche.

Along with the mental stimulation, the other good thing about Harold was that he was an incentive to stay drug-free. When we became an item, he made it very clear that I had to choose: drugs or him.

Choosing him meant putting up with a lot of his putting me down. There were snide remarks about my weight (along with filling up on too much TV, I'd also filled up on way too much food).

For love of Harold, I shed some pounds. That only made him find another point of attack. There were cracks about my being on the way to being a has-been. And I was putting up with this crap, jumping through hoops for this man—*nothing's ever good enough for a Scorpio!* It was like I was punishing myself and had hired him to help. And I thought this was love? When was I going to start living my life for the love of *Chaka*?

Harold and I would have plans to do something and then— something would come up with his daughter and he'd have to bail. Okay, I'd tell myself, you can't begrudge a guy for trying to do his duty as a father. But what's up with the Ex?

I tried to ignore the suspicion that he was playing me against her—running to her rescue at the drop of a hat, and usually when we had plans. I tried to chalk it up to coincidence, to his feeling guilty perhaps, over the impact of their breakup on his daughter. I tried to give him a lot of latitude, but meanwhile I knew I was being abused.

Even on my birthday, he ditched me!

His Ex's birthday was about ten days before mine. And it just so happened that she decided to have her fortieth birthday party on my birthday. So naturally, Harold couldn't spend the evening with me.

I sucked it up, even let him borrow my keyboard when he told me one was needed for her party. And there I was on my birthday, crying my eyes out. I stayed with Harold for way too long. Christmas was approaching when I finally got a grip.

We had plans to go to be together for the holidays but then—wouldn't you know—rain check? His Ex, his daughter, and his Ex's family were spending the holidays in Switzerland. Daddy's little princess wanted him there, too.

"You need to come to England for a couple of days," I told Harold when he returned from Switzerland. Spending time with his Ex and his daughter wasn't the biggest issue. Harold was married to his work. That's what I was really playing second fiddle to.

When he got to my place, I sat his ass down at my kitchen table—"You know I need more. This is not working."

He wasn't willing to give more. I was no longer willing to put up with less.

"Zo how do vee shleep togezer tonight, as brozuh and

sistuh?"

"Yeah," I say, "as brozuh and sistuh."

And, yeah, some of the family, they'd been tsk-tsking, shaking their heads, wondering why I kept getting stuck in romances that netted me misery.

Tammy had come to England a few years after I moved there, but not just to see me. Howard McCrary was uppermost on her mind. The youngest son of his parents' ten children, Howard and two of his sisters and two of his brothers were one of the founding families of contemporary gospel music. When they went into secular music, The McCrary Five often toured with and opened for the Jackson Five. The McCrarys—that sure is one talented family! Howard is a brilliant singer/musician/composer, whose credits include the score for the Broadway hit *Don't Get God Started*. His solo album, *So Good,* was nominated for a Grammy. One of Howard's sons from his first marriage, Darius, made his acting debut in the flick *Big Shots,* and eventually became best known as Eddie Winslow on *Family Matters*. I could go on and on about the fabulous McCrarys, but I won't.

Howard and Tammy had met in the States, at a self-help course called Life Spring in '92. Tammy was searching for which way to go careerwise, after all her years as Miss Goodie Two Shoes. Okay, she wasn't an angel, but compared to the grief Mark, Bonnie, and I gave our mother, Tammy was like Sister Saint. At least Mama had one child who graduated from high school!

As a teen, Tammy had thought of becoming an accountant. By the time she was in her early twenties she knew she wanted to be in entertainment, on the business side. After a year at Cal Berkeley, she transferred to UCLA Extension program, where she took some entertainment business courses. Then, little sister started an image consulting business, Creative Image, partnering up with an ex-girlfriend of Mark's and her sister. Tammy also went into development and management of Milini's group.

It wasn't long after Pretty in Pink folded that Tammy took Life Spring where she met Howard. After she and Howard hit it off, they started talking about her managing his career. They put the talks on hold when he left for a European tour. His last stop was Birmingham, England, which turned out to be where he decided to stay. Howard was having problems in his marriage. When he was offered an extended run at a jazz club in Birmingham, he saw no reason to refuse. So Birmingham became the place Tammy wanted to be, and where she stayed after she and Howard became an item. I got to know Howard even better when we worked together.

Sometime in '95, my new manager David Brokaw (who managed Bill Cosby) told me about a play coming to London's West End that had a character, Sister Carrie, he thought I could play.

Sister Carrie is the wise, world-weary once famous blues singer who is godmother to the central character, Doris Winter, in Vy Higginsen's musical *Mama, I Want to Sing*. Yeah, life is stranger than fiction. I had to laugh. Me playing a former blues singer. Me giving Doris advice on "knowing when to leave the party." Me serving as mediator between Doris and her mother when Doris hits the terrible teens. I had to laugh.

Howard auditioned for the part of Doris's "Jesus," her father, pastor of a church in Harlem, who dies when Doris is a little girl (enter Sister Carrie for the comfort). When Howard got the part, he and Tammy moved to London.

Mama, I Want to Sing was my first full-out experience with gospel. (Remember I am one of the few R&B singers of my generation who didn't come out of the Black Church). Expanding my repertoire was great! Doing theater—HATED IT!

What a killer! It was like a job! It was like ground hog's day. I knew what I would be doing E-V-E-R-Y D-A-Y. When the run was finally over, I literally could not bring myself to even go near that theater. Those three months wore me out.

By then, I was living in a tri-level mews house, where I had more company: Howard and Tammy. Then Mark came across the pond, on his road to recovery.

Mark had continued to work with me after *Chaka*, not as musical director, but as one of my bass players sometimes, in the studio and on the road. He continued contributing tunes, and co-writing some ("Heed the Warning," "What Am I Missing?"), along with doing some background (we sound so much alike!).

We did a lot of shows along the way with jazz drummer Lenny White. Mark became tight with Lenny and his bass player, the future very-major Marcus Miller, who was close to Mark's age.

Mark and Marcus stayed in touch off and on, off and on, then lost touch completely for about two years. We were just coming off the *I Feel for You* tour in '85, when Marcus tracked Mark down in New York, and gave him the 411 on what he and Lenny were up to. Mark was game and in a minute working on the Jamaica Boys' first album *JB,* with the hit "Spend Some Time With Me."

Mark stayed with the Jamaica Boys for a few years, and also did a little freelancing here and there, co-creating "Da Butt" for Spike's *School Daze,* for one. After about four years, the Jamaica Boys had to cut Mark loose, because he had made one too many mess-ups: little brother had followed in big sister's footsteps when it came to drugs and booze.

By now, I recognized that wherever I went my family followed sooner or later. My father was no exception. Around the time he left London, it was Bonnie's turn. She was there when Tammy and Howard married in '95, on a day special to the family: September 8, Gramma Maude's birthday.

Tammy and Howard kept it simple, making it official at the Registry Office in London. Bonnie and I were the witnesses. Other than us, there was a friend of Tammy and Howard, Joseph Houseal, and Bonnie's boyfriend, Tom, whom she had met several years before while in a rehab program in Arizona. A month after Tammy and Howard tied the knot, Bonnie and Tom did the same and in the same place. I was happy for my sisters and wishing them bliss—but did their wedding days send me daydreaming that one day soon I'd remarry? Hell no!

Tammy and Howard had planned to stay in London, but

ended up rushing back to the States when Howard's father, age 82, suffered a mild heart attack. Once in L.A., they decided they wanted to stay close to family and L.A. remained their home, where in '97 and '00 they had their sons, Tallon and Tyler.

Before Howard and Tammy left England, I had decided to let Tammy be my personal manager. By then, she was managing Howard.

It was a dream come true for Tammy. Since high school she had wanted to be my manager. During my insane New York days, sixteen-year-old Tammy had written a letter to our mother explaining why she needed to move to New York to take care of Milini and Damien (and me, too, I guess!). She proposed finishing high school by correspondence course. My mother laughed her butt to bed. Together, Tammy and I decided to create the management company, Raeven Productions.

My baby sister, Zaheva, also came to London at one point, as part of her search for direction. (She passed on the entertainment business and eventually decided on law school.) Zaheva was part of the crew that went with me to South Africa in '94.

I'd been approached about working in South Africa in the past. As long as apartheid ruled my answer was, "No." Once apartheid ended, I was open, very much so when a black South African promoter approached me about a tour (two shows in Johannesburg, two in Durban, two in Capetown). It was one of the very first shows promoted by a black South African. I was so jazzed to be a part of a new day South Africa.

The negotiations went smoothly and all of the business was

handled properly. Things got a little weird about a week before we were set to leave: the second half of the fee didn't arrive as promised. The promoter promised he'd deliver when we arrived. I was fine with that. After all, the guy had footed the bill for airfare and lodgings of the many people I wanted to make this journey with me. In addition to my musicians, singers, Simone, and other staff members, there was Aunt Barbara, Zaheva, Tammy, Mark, Damien, Harold (this was before we broker up), Tammy's Howard, and my dear friend Pepsi.

When I arrived in South Africa—no lie, the feeling was akin to an orphaned child meeting her biological mother for the first time. That was my first time in the Motherland I'd learned about and sung about during my Affro-Arts days.

It saddened me to see apartheid wasn't all the way dead. As I found out, the promoter was fighting a losing battle. He was being sabotaged at every turn—in advertising, venue costs, and even record company support. Long story short: he was elbowed out by a white South African promoter after the first show in Johannesburg. (And I never did the full plan of shows.)

Workwise the trip was a semi-disaster. But I could never regret the journey. Most memorable was the time I spent in Soweto. So many people so poverty-stricken, and yet they showed so much love—not only to us but to their neighbors who'd been so vicious to them and their ancestors. I saw— live!—the great power of the human spirit. I saw love triumphing over hate.

Beautiful, too, was spending time with one of my earliest musical mentors, Miriam Makeba, and making friends with another amazing South African artist, Yvonne Chaka Chaka!

That was not my only trip to South Africa. Later in the '90s, I did an AIDS benefit show in Johannesburg, with Stevie Wonder and a bunch of other great artists. Once again, the invite came from black South African promoter—this time it was President Mandela's daughter, Zinzi. It was a huge event and very well promoted. More wonderful than all that was an invitation to President Mandela's home. Meeting that awesome man was one of the most humbling and inspiring experiences of my life.

My greatest adventure while living in Europe was my house!

Tammy had been helping me look for a house when she was still living in Birmingham. During one of her trips to London, she came upon a six bedroom, four bath red-brick Edwardian in West Hampstead.

The owner was a sad old lady living in one or two rooms, with space heaters—family gone, husband dead—the rest of the house occupied by boarders. But it would be a BEAUTIFUL house I knew—once you got past the many layers of wallpaper and the thick coats of paint over beautiful natural wood doors and over the antique fireplaces in nearly every room. Once we ripped up the carpet-over-linoleum-over-carpet—there were once-beautiful golden pine floors. When the house got new windows, new doors, and a wall knocked down so I could have a master bath connected to the master bedroom. . . . In other words, once I did a full-out renovation.

My bathroom's pride were the bathtub, toilet, and double sink, in gorgeous Old World red marble. A gift from Harold (this was before we broke up). While making a documentary in Bordeaux, he came upon a castle being demolished. He rescued the red marble bath set, and had it shipped to me, knowing I'd love it. (I guess he wasn't all bad!)

I did my bedroom in an African Savannah motif, which included a Jaguar over my door, sweeping in as though from a tree branch. For my bath, I chose a Dracula motif. Kenya meets Transylvania? They actually worked pretty well together.

I had my own "Michaelangos": two German friends, Michael and Angela, created frescoes in my bathroom and bedroom, in one of the upstairs bedrooms, and in other small parts of the house. Bonnie and I painted every room of the house a different color—and, yes, we had the skills. We were our mother's daughters when it came to that.

I planted wisteria in the front of the house and an herb garden in back.

It was for the love of that house (and overseeing the renovation) that I'd rented the mews house. It was close by.

Chaka "United-Nations" Khan. That's what some friends called me when it came to me and men. They had even more reason to do so when I hooked up with a Korean guy born in Japan. Something to do with his having a record label is how Bonnie came to know him, and then he came to know me, and developed a humongous crush.

I didn't think I was rebounding when I took Sangki up on his offer to love me true. He had been pursuing me for a while. He had come to see *Mama, I Want to Sing* damn near every night. And every single time, he came with flowers and praise. I don't know how he got my number but once he did he called and called and after a while I thought . . . *Sangki is really sweet.*

"You are my queen." Everlasting love he claimed it would be.

Okay, if he loves me that much I'll give it a shot.

That man would give me anything, do anything for me—anything he thought might make me happy. If I had a gig in the States or somewhere else out of England, he thought nothing of flying to wherever I had to be. He could afford it, and indulged his fever to satisfy my every wish and whim (along with wishes and whims I didn't even have) because he had a lot of money: from his record business; plus, his family owned a lot of gambling halls in Japan.

By '98, I was feeling the need to move again. Demands of work, and potential work meant my needing to be back in the States. I had no problem with the shift, because wherever I've moved, no matter how much I've adored a place—and I certainly loved my London house—I never felt it was permanent. I've always stayed committed to going with my flow. Did I sell the house? Nope. I may live there again one day, for a time. In the meantime, Bonnie and her husband live there.

Along with work, there was the matter of my children. They

wanted to live close to me, if not with me. They had visited me a few times in London but when I tried to get them to move there, they were like, *No way!*

When I left London, I landed in L.A., crashed at my mother's while I figured out where I wanted to be. New York called, but I thought about how crowded it was, how they wanted crazy money for apartments, and how the city had worn me the hell out. In the end, I decided that while I wouldn't live in New York, I'd live close to it.

I ended up with this big crazy ass house with land forever in Alpine, New Jersey. I thought it was too big for me, but the kids loved it, so I went on and got it. Over the years I'd done a lot of that: letting them have what they wanted, out of guilt. Over the years—thousands and thousands and thousands dollars worth of toys, clothes, money, cars. And freedom.

So there I was in Alpine, in too much house, with Milini and I going through some typical mother-daughter stuff. Milini had always found fault with aspects of my lifestyle—above and beyond the drugging. She was very opinionated, vocal as hell. But I had raised both my children to be that way. (Damien, however, was never as judgmental).

But in Alpine we had some great times. When the weather was warm, we had monster barbecues—my friends, their friends, their friends' friends. We had a lot of easy, simple pleasures, like all of us going to malls (we shopped a lot!). And there was watching TV with Raeven, taking Raeven to a skating rink or zoo, applauding Raeven's singing and dancing, dancing and singing, coming again and again to my bedroom to put on a show. I had to be the MC.

"Ladies and gentlemen, presenting . . ." We'd make up some kind of name—Shanequa Finesse, Shanika Alissa—and then Raeven would come out "on stage," sometimes in some of my clothes. And she'd sing and dance, dance and sing. She wore me out with her shows. But I wouldn't have missed one for the world.

When I moved to Alpine, it quickly became Sangki's favorite destination, and he kept being so sweet, so giving, so smothering me with too damn much of his love! Too many gifts!

He didn't want to take "no more" for an answer. He persisted, insisted we had to be forever, no matter what I said to him. Finally, I told him there were things in his life he had to get together. For one, I felt really strongly that he needed to go find that almost-grown child he had fathered with a woman in Japan and never once laid eyes on. I thought how that boy must have felt having Anonymous for a father.

"Go find your son now! You really need to find your son!"

He made like he had tried and the trail had gone cold.

"Then, you weren't looking all that hard! You can find him. The way you pursued me I know you can find anything."

Sangki went looking for his son. He found him too late. Calling from Japan, he was hysterical as he told me that about a week before he discovered his son's whereabouts, the boy's mother had killed him. Then, herself. In a society where an out-of-wedlock birth is regarded as a mega-shame, the ostracism his child's mother had been up against had, apparently, pushed her over the edge.

I tried to be as loving, as gentle as I could with Sangki. I really felt how awful he felt, but if he thought his sorrow would convince me to stay with him, I couldn't, I couldn't. Then, it all became a non-issue shortly after he returned to England from Japan. En route to meet two guys interested in buying his label, he was in a car crash and burned to death.

That was a death I certainly wasn't ready for. I was devastated, and I said to myself, "Chaka, you need to do a time-out on men."

20

MASTERJAM

Way back when, we had both said if we ever got free, we'd get together for a very special jam.

The talent born Prince Roger Nelson later known as Prince, aka , aka The Artist Formerly Known As Prince, aka TAFKAP, aka The Artist (whew!) had gotten his freedom from Warner in '95 and gone on to launch his own recording label, New Power Generation Records, in '96.

I completely understood why he had walked around with S-L-A-V-E on his face. I was feeling it!

He had supplied the visual commentary. In a few years, at a Digital Hollywood conference, Courtney Love would supply the "narrative," with her "Manifesto" (or diatribe as some called it), which I drop here in part:

I want to start with a story about rock bands and record companies, and do some recording-contract math:

This story is about a bidding-war band that gets a huge deal with a 20 percent royalty rate and a million-dollar advance. (No bidding-war band ever got a 20 percent royalty, but whatever.) . . .

What happens to that million dollars?

They spend half a million to record their album. That leaves the band with $500,000. They pay $100,000 to their manager for 20 percent commission. They pay $25,000 each to their lawyer and business manager.

That leaves $350,000 for the four band members to split. After $170,000 in taxes, there's $180,000 left. That comes out to $45,000 per person.

That's $45,000 to live on for a year until the record gets released.

The record is a big hit and sells a million copies. (How a bidding-war band sells a million copies of its debut record is another rant entirely . . .)

So, this band releases two singles and makes two videos. The two videos cost a million dollars to make and 50 percent of the video production costs are recouped out of the band's royalties.

The band gets $200,000 in tour support, which is 100 percent recoupable.

The record company spends $300,000 on independent radio promotion. You have to pay independent promotion to get your song on the radio; independent promotion is a system where the record companies use middlemen so they can pretend not to know that radio stations . . . are getting paid to play their records.

All of those independent promotion costs are charged to the band.

Since the original million-dollar advance is also re-coupable, the band owes $2 million to the record company.

If all of the million records are sold at full price with no discounts or record clubs, the band earns $2 million in royalties, since their 20 percent royalty works out to $2 a record.

Two million dollars in royalties minus $2 million in re-coupable expenses equals . . . zero!

How much does the record company make?

According to Love, the company grossed $11 million. She then minused expenses—half million to make the CDs; the band's advance of $1 million; $1 million for making the videos; $300,000 in radio promotion; $200,000 in tour support; $750,000 for publishing royalties; $2.2 million for marketing—for a net profit of $6.6 million.

Of course, [the band] had fun. Hearing yourself on the radio, selling records, getting new fans and being on TV is great, but now the band doesn't have enough money to pay the rent and nobody has any credit.

Worst of all, after all this, the band owns none of its

work. . . .

When you look at the legal line on a CD, it says copyright 1976 Atlantic Records or copyright 1996 RCA Records. When you look at a book, though, it'll say something like copyright 1999 Susan Faludi, or David Foster Wallace. Authors own their books and license them to publishers. When the contract runs out, writers gets their books back. But record companies own our copyrights forever.

The system's set up so almost nobody gets paid.

I not only wanted to get paid. I wanted to be free to do music the way I wanted to do it. I'd had it with the control, the manipulation, the spin. And they were good, they were very, very good to the point that at times they had me questioning myself—Am I a good singer? Am I chopped liver? Am I a piece of—

Then I'd hear my voice. I knew my voice. I'd hear what I can do—I'd think back to times I'd been sick as a dog and the show went on because when I get into that zone, into that spiritual place where my voice lives, I detach from my body. I'd hear my voice and . . . Some Warner execs wanted me to believe that without them I was nothing.

Warner was going through a lot of changes, including a lot of personnel changes. By the mid-'90s, I hardly knew anybody there anymore. And they had the nerve to give me an A&R person who could have been my daughter! True, age is "just a number." There was no harm in her being young, per se. But I just didn't seem to get what I was all about. *How dare this child dictate to ME what material I should use on my CD!*

And where do they come off telling ME how to sing the songs!—"Can you take this next album a little more Faithesque or Mary J-esque."

"Come on, mutha—Look, you want Faith and Mary J.? Then go get them!"

After I recorded a damn fine CD of great songs, *Dare You to Love Me,* their response was, "We think you need to go back into the studio and record six more."

But I heard my voice! I was no novice! I had been in the business for nearly twenty-five years! Nobody, but nobody was as demanding, as hard on Chaka as Chaka! Every track, every album, I'm competing with myself, reaching for higher. And sure enough after a song comes out, invariably, I hit on something I could have done differently, better. One of my nightmares is listening to a song one, three, ten years down the road, and thinking, "What the hell was I on?"

But THEY thought I needed to go back into the studio and record six more.

No!

So Warner kicked the CD to the curb: "not commercial enough." Yeah, I'd give them *enough* alright.

I requested a meeting with Warner's bossman. I asked for emancipation.

We struck a deal. They asked for one more album—and a wait-and-see approach until that April. If, by then, I was still not satisfied with the treatment they were giving me, they would let me walk.

"Free and clear? You'll just let me go?"

Free and clear, they promised.

I could see their lawyer, wanting to kick himself (or somebody else). And I didn't miss the cocky, dismissive tone they took with me, as if I was bluffing, hysterical, being temperamental—as if I'd be too scared to leave them. They could think what they wanted to think, but I had made a point of coming to the meeting with witnesses—my lawyer included.

This was in late fall '95. After the meeting, I started brainstorming on the CD I'd give them. I settled on a greatest hits collection, with a few songs Warner was happy with from *Dare You to Love Me,* for the making of *Epiphany.*

April came. And I came in from London, with my witnesses, to meet with the Warner suits again. I let them know that I was still not satisfied with the treatment I was getting, and that I had not been bluffing.

"I want to go, I want to walk."

I'd kept my end of the bargain and Warner kept theirs. I was free.

Where was I going? I didn't have a clue. Starting my own record label was on my wish list, but I knew making that dream come true would take more than a minute. In the meantime, I had my road work, and I was loving my life in London. So, in the meantime, I gave myself permission to be a free agent. As often happens when we take a gamble, it wasn't all that long before a great opportunity came along.

In the winter of '98, I was in Minneapolis. The Artist and I had finally come together for the making of what would be *Come 2 My House.*

It was a work of love as well as trust. We did it all without contracts. Word was bond. It wasn't about who was in control. We'd each own our stuff. It was all about the music, giving our talents free reign. Our motto: "Come Real." We promised each other this would be the beginning of a new way of doing music. We were out to start a movement.

Our concept for this first CD was an extended love song: a journey into the stages, facets, phases, of an intense romance.

"Give me some tracks, I'll write some lyrics."

"No," said The Artist. To start, he wanted me to produce some poems.

With my long history of making music in the reverse—letting the music draw me to the verse—I had no idea writing the words first could work so well for me. I was more honest, more open.

"I want you to write your life story in a poem," he said one evening.

That night I began to reflect on this crazy life of mine, and the next day I hit him with my memories:

As a little girl, I had a stubborn mind
Bonnie and I were wild most of the time
I used 2 sing 4 mama's company
I guess that was the start of the woman I came 2 b

And my reflections:

> *Never will forget from whence I came*
> *I have some regrets, but I made myself a name*
> *2 times a mother and as many times wed*
> *Tough times around me, but better times ahead. . . .*

The next day he hit me with the music.

He was fast and he trusted himself, never second guessed a move—and that takes a lot of balls. That's genius in itself.

Out popped poem after poem with able assists from people so special to me: brother Mark, brother-in-law Howard, Robert Palmer, Kirk Johnson, Sandra St. Victor, Larry Graham, and of course The Artist.

"We need the breaking-up part," he said at one point.

The floodgates opened up. I rewound to my time with Harold. I came up with "The Drama."

> *In this ever-changing world*
> *Where things become unfurled*
> *and tethered*
> *Like a lioness in her pride*
> *I was gonna stay by your side*
> *4ever. . . .*

The Artist and I had very little conversation about the music. Usually, we hit the studio about four in the afternoon, and started running our mouths, signifying, eating, until maybe eight or so, then got in about three hours of work.

It was almost like working with myself. We definitely had the hook-up. I hadn't done so much writing since my days with Rufus.

Sometimes, in the interest of keeping it real, we switched up: with "Spoon," first came the tune.

One day The Artist turned me on to a song he'd created for Spike Lee's, *Girl 6*, "Don't Talk 2 Strangers." I was there. I wanted that song in my *House*. No, I'd never been bound for jail giving a good-bye to my kids. But I had been gone, that's for sure. Even then, I truly did believe that one day everything, everything, everything would be alright

> *Don't talk 2 strangers*
> *Don't 4get 2 say your prayers at night*
> *Remember God—He made U*
> *and one day He'll make everything alright. . . .*

"What's next?" I'd just knocked out a song.

"We're finished."

I didn't want it to be over! I really loved working with him. True, I never enjoyed flying up to freezing Minnesota (I wasn't feeling that!) but once we were working I stayed jazzed.

It's frightening how fast it all happened, how everybody was so in sync: with Tom Tucker doing most of the mix and Clare Fischer arranging the strings with such strength just as he did during my Rufus years. And there was Queen Latifah "dropping by" to rap for "Pop My Clutch," and Brother Jules to scratch for "Betcha." Larry Graham was so central on so much, especially with his touch-up on the finer points of "Hair." They and so many other tight talents surrendered their all for this jam. Some definite magic got made at Paisley Park Studios in a fast two or three weeks if you bunched all the time together.

"Since Chaka Khan first dropped her flavor in the early Seventies, her influence has spread exponentially, affecting singers who don't even know they're biting her style," began a *Rolling Stone* review of *Come 2 My House*. "Her voice is an instrument of knowingness, carnality, spirituality and intellect. On *Come 2 My House*, co-written and co-produced with the Artist for his NPG label, the voice is better than ever. If melted caramel had a sound, this would be it: rich, thick, warm and enveloping."

". . . and it's as funky as you could hope for," wrote David Betrand Wilson, "fat bass, gutsy horns (by the Hornheadz), solid riffs that somehow never sound derivative ("I'll Never Be Another Fool"), crazy touches like the title track's heavy breathing-meets-jazz piano. Studio gadgets are used to add interest and excitement, not as crutches or ploys for commercial acceptance. . . . Khan's voice is always given plenty of room, and several tracks feature that "Wall of Chakas". . . . There are also several choice ballads: "Remember U," "Journey 2 The Center Of Your Heart," which for some reason has been lying in 's vault for years. Larry Graham drops by on a remake of his hit "Hair," but stays in the background so that the track is a statement about individualism instead of just a bass showcase."

". . . [O]n this certified masterpiece," wrote *Vibe*, "Chaka finally manifests all the lyric, emotional, improvisational mastery we always knew she was capable of. Thirteen poems given flesh by the New Power Generation's voodoo conjurations, *Come 2 My House* is both a reaffirmation of faith and an artistic maturation."

"Not since her days with Rufus has Khan been pushed to such fiercely funky heights as on her first release on the Artist's NPG label," remarked *USA Today.*

Not every review was a rave through and through but a lot of people got it—saw what we had been doing, thought we had offered up something worthy.

Larry Graham had summed up this baby so well: "What you hear on this album is freedom. Chaka was free to do what she wanted to do. If she didn't like something, she could change it without having to worry about studio costs or anything else. There were no restrictions."

Except in the marketplace, as in, "if a tree falls in the forest and nobody hears it, does it make a sound?" Damn!

When it came to the marketing and promotion, we seriously miscalculated. We thought we'd get a lot of mileage out of our existing status and the novelty of what we'd done.

We hung a lot of our hope on our touring with Larry Graham, but that got put on eternal hold after The Artist and I had a couple of mishaps on stage, that left both of us lame for a while. Damn!

But what a glorious time I had with the Artist—so affirming! The Artist had treated me like a straight brother. He really took care of me—gave me a handsome advance. When I left Warner I had had no place to go. I had my road work, but

I needed to invest in my future and give my fans new music. And The Artist was there for me. He bottom-lined *Come 2 My House* all the way: I had no costs. Not one! I really loved him for that, for putting his money where his mouth was. You don't meet many people like that.

I still regard *Come 2 My House* as my best album to date. So you can understand how crushed I was that it didn't really get out there, and ended up being an album people recall as a masterjam that never got its props.

On the upside, I gained a whole new respect for the financial commitment it takes to promote an album properly, and for what record companies do when they support an artist's album.

21

EPIPHANY

This isn't you!

It was July something-or-other. I had always partied like it was 1999 and now it finally was. A sticky wicked time.

Carmel-coated pseudo happy
Call her sticky wicked
Will she answer agin today or pray that love'll kick it?

I had a lot of help getting sticky wicked with yet another "Mr. Right." A handsome self-made man with his own small business.

"I've got *just* the right man for you!" Aunt Kathy had boasted when she talked me into saying okay to a blind dinner date at her place. Aunt Kathy had been living in L.A. for some time.

When I met the guy Aunt Kathy was so keen on, true to form, it was love at first sight. I fell fast and hard. This guy seemed like a real man and he was the first black man I'd been with in a long, long time.

"The Grammy Award–winning songstress," people had read in *Jet,* "who has dated White men in the past, noted that a lot of Black men could not handle the pressures of her fame or her being a breadwinner." Whether all the white men I'd been with had made the grade on this account the writer hadn't bothered to ask—this writer I let know I was thinking of making a baby with this Mr. Right. Did I mention he loved keeping me full of crack?

This isn't you!

Kick it love, visions of her childhood
When her heart was gold
Sticky wicked
Tell me people what reason's good enough 2
Die before U're old? Kick it love, covenants of promise
lay before your eyes
Stick wicked will trick U, lick U, then it kicks you aside!

It was early afternoon. I was in my apartment in Venice. It wasn't that Alpine, New Jersey, had gotten on my nerves, but I thought it was time to let my kids start standing on their own two feet. I didn't really kick them out of the nest. I left them in the house, with Patsy, a woman I hired to play surrogate mother—to help out with cooking, cleaning, be nanny to Raeven, and keep a watch out. Then I brought my butt back to California, and dropped in Venice because that's where "Mr. Right" lived.

Yeah, I've sometimes wondered how some people live in the same damn place all their lives and are happy. Even in my right mind, I think I'd get a headache if I tried to make a list of all my moves.

But I had more than a headache on that July afternoon in '99. I was struggling to get clear, to come out of the fog of something deeper but less restful than sleep, after yet another all-nighter of binge drugging and drinking.

I was hungry as hell and thirsty, too. But uppermost on my mind was copping—scoring again and again and . . .

This isn't you! This is not you, Yvette!

Of all the shameful things I've done (and I know there are plenty I don't remember), one incident stands out as one of the most shameful and painful. The memory of this incident smacked me in the face that July afternoon. It was something I'd recently done to some children in Compton, during a program Tammy had gotten me involved in.

People crashing in the middle of the day
When U wake up sticky wicked don't go away
Sticky wicked
Pretty stick wicked

Tammy had seen the signs of a dip, feared a spiral was coming when all my hopes for *Come 2 My House* ended up in ashes. Tammy had recently met someone she came to trust and respect: Reverend Alfreddie Johnson, founder of the World Literacy Crusade (WLC), doing worthy work to build up needy children and adults. Tammy and Howard had met Reverend Johnson at a function. In talking with him, one thing led to the other, and Tammy and Howard joined Johnson's True Faith Christian Center.

When Tammy reached out to Johnson for ways to help me help myself, they came up with a plan. This plan was rooted in Johnson's belief that overcoming problems is bound up in helping others overcome theirs. Once Tammy told him about my concern for children, especially children in or on the rim of crisis, they refined the plan.

First, he called, and we talked and I let him into my life. He saw things in me that I was afraid to see, didn't want to acknowledge for so long, because when you really know something you have to do something about it. It gets harder to hide, harder to take pride in living in the moment.

He told me there's a power in me. He urged me to turn the power to good. Rev summed me up as "an eagle hanging out with chickens. "

"Chaka, you have the power to lead people to light. Or to hell."

Quick, he and his second, Dr. Hanan, came to see me. They weren't starstruck. They didn't get tripping over being in the presence of Cha-ka Khan, Cha-ka Khan. They were no strangers to stars. All they saw was a woman in crisis, no different from other women they'd reached out to over the years. Only difference was that in most cases all I had on those women was fame which ain't worth shit when you're living like you ain't got shit to live for—when you're struggling to burn away ugly memories and shame. Not to mention feeling crushed sometimes by the burden you feel because the livelihoods and luxuries of so many people you love are hitched to your star . . . Poor me.

Rev and Dr. Hanan tough-loved me. They got my attention, got me to get dressed, and out of my apartment. They told me there was something that needed doing that I could do.

We hit an art store, picked up a bunch of art supplies, then headed to WLC. Rev had put out a call for kids interested in art to beat it to over there ASAP.

I fell in love with the work WLC was doing in a heartbeat. I fell in love with the children, too, and the Chaka Khan Art Club was born. I agreed to go to WLC twice a week to teach children to draw and to paint.

"Like an artist with no art form, she became dangerous." Toni Morrison had captured a truth so well, so right. Of course, I am living proof that an artist with her art form can also become dangerous. But anyway, I knew how therapeutic, how healing art can be. What with the slashing of funds for art programs in public schools, a WLC art program for these Compton kids was all the more necessary.

Through art, I helped them create, express their fears and longings, get a break from "daddy's-maybe," the gang shit, the schools that are like holding pens because teachers and admins figure the children are on their way to prison anyway. Through art, perhaps these children could catch onto a positive dream.

Their adoration was pure, and that first week was so wonderful, as was the second, third, fourth, fifth . . . But week six, I showed up in an altered state.

The children were all eyes.

"What's up with that? . . ."

"She tripping. . . ."

They giggled, whispered.

I felt so naked, so awfully wrong.

The memory of that moment came flooding back strong that July afternoon.

Why didn't I just call in sick? Who did I think I'd fool? How could I have done that to the children! They know high when they see it—they see it all the time—

Hey little baby, what's your name?
Oh ain't she cute?
Mama got 2 run today
I don't have time 4 games
No don't worry about me, I'm alright
I'm alright, I'm alright

—and that's NOT what they needed to see from you! Enough Yvette!

I'd always been able to pull myself back from the brink in the nick of time—but I was tired of ending up at the brink in the first damn place.

You deserve better than this, Yvette.

Tammy had been researching places where I could get clear. Someone told her about a super sauna detox program. At the Scientology Celebrity Center.

Tammy did a step back, but she held onto the information and remained curious. Then, because the Scientology Celebrity Center's Purification Program isn't just for junkies, but for anyone wanting to cleanse of anything—environmental toxins, pharmaceuticals, stress—she decided to do a test run with Howard. They found it an amazing experience.

Rev. was also an advocate of the program. It took a little convincing because, like Tammy, I did a step back. Just wrapping my head around getting clean was about as much as I could handle. And I had no interest in signing on for Scientology. But after Tammy said it was cool—no strings attached—I decided to give it a shot.

You can lead people to light. Or to Hell.

Every day for many, many weeks, I lived at the Château Elysée in Hollywood. I spent long hours in the sauna, knocking back heavy-duty vitamins, eating wholesome all-natural foods. There was the working out, working out—more sweating it out, day by day getting closer to getting clear.

All sorts of drugs oozed from me, even some vestiges of something from recent dental work—leaving me with the mother of all toothaches for about a week, and I couldn't take anything for it—no aspirin, no nothing, but music. Honest, healing music. A lot of Joni. K.d. lang's *Ingénue* became a constant. Practically every day, while in the sauna or walking the treadmill I listened to that CD over and over again—"Constant Craving"... "Season of Hollow Soul"... "Outside Myself"... "Tears of Love's Recall"... "Wash Me Clean"... "Save Me"... "So It Shall Be."

For years, I lied to myself, wanted to believe that I was alright because I was just a spotter, and always did my herbal mojo to build back up. As if not being high *every* day meant you didn't have a problem, as if not recognizing that I was one hell of an escape artist wasn't one hell of a problem.

Coming off a tour I'd come home and just leave myself, leave my body for a week. Escape. And when things got weird, crazy... the kids wanting more time with me, the kids cursing out Mama, the kids keeping me in a ring of guilt about me being *gone*, about me being high, about me not fooling them—they knew half the time it was really Mama who bought their birthday and Christmas presents, because I didn't have time for that, time to read them bedtime stories, time to sit Milini down and tell her about Hassan—running, running, running from the truth... leaving Milini to wonder why she didn't see herself—her eyes, her nose, her mouth—in my family, in Rahsaan's family—leaving her to be broadsided by the news at age fourteen, courtesy of Hassan. Escape. I'd just check out. When I couldn't take Mama and Tammy piling on more guilt, when their worrying only made me feel worse—escape. When I let people force me into doing things I didn't want to do—escape. Like filing bankruptcy... Living too large, having a tour or two that put me in the red—I would have been fine to keep ducking and dodging, paying bills off as I could, but I didn't because I let myself be so micro-managed, let other people convince me they knew best, like *I* was a fool . . . My need to escape from feeling alone, never feeling I truly had anyone to shoulder some of the burden, to listen to me, hear my cries about how confused I got sometimes and why again and again I took up with men who were no good for me . . . In search of my father, perhaps . . . and because women aren't allowed to be alone, to feel okay if they ain't got a man and then you get one and you're hoping for love but you get jealousy and bullshit, betrayals, and drugs and him and other people thinking you're a slut because you're on the road with a band full of men so you must be screwing each and every one of them . . . And being on the road, so always on the move . . . Meeting someone who might make a good-good friend but you know you can't cultivate that, can't maintain because you have to move on, to escape from knowing you're a lousy mother to escape from friends and so-called friends coming to you for advice, leaning on you, laying all their problems on you, making you their guru—because *Chaka is strong, Chaka is tough, Chaka don't take no stuff, Chaka got it going on.*

I'd anticipated the soul-searching—had planned on it in fact. What I was not prepared for was sometimes coming out of the sauna feeling stoned. Evidently, I had to go back to go forward. (I later found out athletes detoxing from steroids sometimes slip into 'roid rage in the sauna and heavy acid users start tripping.)

Along with the soul work and the diet work there was the mind work as well. "Handling Life's Ups and Downs" was the

name of the course, a big part of which was identifying antagonists—the people and forces—that held me back, jammed me
up.

Like the press. While the press had always been pretty good
to me, I recognized that the press was nonetheless an antago-
nistic force. I needed to get better about when to say, "This interview is over." I also needed to get a little better about
thinking before I answered a question.

And there are the fans, the multitude of fans who give me so
much love, and to whom I owe so much. So often, they'd ap-
plaud me for giving my all in a show. But then, after the show,
it didn't occur to them that I might be too exhausted to give
five, twenty, fifty thousand autographs. *Chaka's strong!* Not always. Not 24/7. And a lot of people just don't understand that,
yes, I love what I do, but what I do is *work,* too.

As for the recording industry—no surprise there. I came to
terms with the fact that it might always be a foe to some extent,
given the realities—the competition, the emphasis on the
bottom line. But, hey, I was doing something I loved. I realized
that to make a living (and a good one at that) doing what you
love is a luxury many people do not have. It was half-past time
for me stop merely venting about what was so wrong with the
recording industry and start putting more energy into what I
could do right within it, if I were going to stay in this business.

Is it the business I'm in with its feverish pace? I wondered at
one point. Is stardom one gigantic mind fuck? Is there something in the artistic "gene"? Is the line between creativity and
madness really that thin?

Would Van Gogh have died with both ears on had he been born with a banker's brain? Would Bird and Miles have lived into lucid old age had they become carpenters? On the other hand, pilots fly drunk, housewives have boozy afternoons, stock brokers snort coke, bankers pop pills. Maybe there's something wrong with most all of us. Maybe Thoreau was right. Maybe most men, most women "live lives of quiet desperation"—and "go to the grave with the song still in them"?

But "most all of us" couldn't be my concern right then. I had to figure *myself* out. Had I missed out on my true song?

First on the list of antagonists—before the media, the recording industry, the demands of stardom—first on the list was Chaka. I never had a lot of love for myself.

The Celebrity Center offered counselors, but I declined one. I didn't want anybody asking me any questions, especially not a stranger. It was hard enough for me to talk honestly with myself. And if I did want to talk face to face with anyone, I had Damien.

We were on the phone one day when I broached the subject, told him I thought given his abuse of weed and booze, the Purif would do him good. And he came, so did his girlfriend Dana (who wasn't a substance abuser). And that was nice, because Dana and I got to bond.

As I welcomed Dana closer into my life, I knew there were many others I'd have to shed. I recognized that some wouldn't understand, that they'd continue to pursue a friendship. For them, I'd be dissing good memories. "Hey, Chaka, remember the time we were doing . . ."

"Yeah, yeah, I remember," I will say whether or not I do, because to deny will only open up that can of worms, empower tattletales and gossips to speculate on how high and out of it I must have been. So, it's easier to just say, "Yeah, yeah, I remember."

After the Purification Program, I had the strength to tell my children: "I'm not here to try to feel guilty about my life with you or the lack of life we had together. We can try to have a life now."

As for myself, during and after Purif I began trying to figure out what it is to love oneself. Where does love end and narcissism begin? Then I figured perhaps the start isn't to know whether or not I love myself, but to treat myself in a good way. Love isn't a feeling or a knowing, after all, but action. So I started working on treating myself well, being as nice to myself as I could be.

All my life I'd been on this quest for freedom. And there I was in my late forties realizing that freedom was the one thing I had always denied myself. Oh, sure, I was good at cut-and-run, at escaping, but that's not freedom.

I discovered my freedom is in the simplest things. Sometimes it's doing nothing, which for me is equivalent to a room full of gold. Now, if I'm on the road and I have a day between travels, or between shows, I allow myself to be free—Do Not Disturb. Unless there's some emergency, I allow no one to make demands on me, for my advice, for my opinion on a business

214

matter, for nada. Things can wait. Looking back, I realize I was on the verge of getting a grip on what freedom for me really is during my early days in London, but then I let my life get too crowded, again.

> *Understand you will not see me down*
> *Both of my feet are on the ground*
> *Come and lay your head upon my chest*
> *I'll love you hard, I'll do my best*

After the Purification Program, whenever I sang "I'm a Woman," I did so with a new dimension. That last verse became one of my mantras. The song's "you" is Yvette.

CODA

Sun . . .
How can I thank you
You've warmed my heart and soul
You've made my body brown and smooth
Washed away the cold

I was about twenty when I wrote these lyrics with my Austrian friend Traude Sapik. (God rest her soul.)

Moon . . .
You've made a dreamer out of me
I can see, and I think I can feel it when you
Change your face . . .

This song, which landed on *Ask Rufus*, was my ode to Creation.

Stars . . .

What a mystical woman that you made me

I've seen of times before the human race

As long as I'm breathing

As long as I can move

I'll be strong . . .

I titled it "Earth Song."

When I decided to start my own record label in '98 I named the company Earth Song Entertainment. With Earth Song, I vowed to give the universe good, true, *honest* music. I also vowed never to exploit a fellow artist—never do anything to anyone I wouldn't want done to me! (For one, I vowed artists would own their own masters.)

While I was on my crack "hiatus," my record label languished, of course. After I got clean, Earth Song became a top priority.

One of the best business decisions I made was to ask my mother to be my business manager/accountant. Over the years, I'd had my share of managers and accountants who were, at times, shall we say, more generous to themselves than to me. But that was something I had to take responsibility for—you know, as in "fool me once shame on you, fool me twice . . ."

My finances were pretty much always a wreck. I'd work my butt off—recording, touring, club gigs, special events—and end up with very little to show for it. For one, I'd spend a lot of money on a whim. I was also careless in small ways, too (and the little things add up!).

"Yvette, you don't have to give the brother a fifty."

That was Mark one day back in the '80s. We were in New York going I don't remember where when a homeless guy asked, "Can you spare a little something so I can get something to eat?" When I reached into my pocketbook, a Ben Franklin was the first thing that came to hand. Thanks to Mark, I switched up to a Lincoln. But there were times when neither Mark nor anyone else with good sense was with me when a panhandler made a plea.

When it came to getting ripped off by people who supposedly worked for me—yeah, I'd heard legions of stories about singers, musicians—all varieties of artists—getting taken by their "people"—managers, accountants, agents, lawyers. But I was too caught up with my drugging and drinking and dramas to put serious energy into scrutinizing my money matters and not getting flimflammed.

When young artists ask me about career dos and don'ts, "You might want to get a law degree," I sometimes advise. Well, perhaps that's a bit extreme. But they should at least take pains to not let anyone hurry them into signing a contract. I advise all young artists to develop the patience to read a contract—to make sure they understand what they're agreeing to before they lay down their John Hancock. Above all, I tell them to be eagle-eyed when it comes to anyone handling their money and giving them financial advice.

Having Tammy as my personal manager revealed what a difference it makes when you have folks who truly love you—and are honest!—at the top of your team. It wasn't just about having people who wouldn't steal from me; there was also the issue of having people who would not hustle me into decisions on gigs and other business matters out of their own self-interest.

As I worked on Earth Song's infrastructure, I also worked on product. I was working in the studio in late 2000, when I met Douglas Rasheed.

My engineer had suggested I take a listen to some of Doug's tracks. I didn't know anything about the guy other than that he was a co-writer of "Gangsta's Paradise." I liked that song the moment I heard it. And I liked the material Doug brought to Earth Song. And then, wouldn't you know it, I started really liking Doug . . . The feeling was mutual.

No, Chaka, a man is the last thing you need right now. Stay focused on your work! But there was something special about Doug.

With every guy there's always been something special and what has it gotten you? But during our first conversation we *talked*—Doug hadn't been flooding me with flattery or otherwise trying to supe me up. He had been himself, it seemed.

But which self? People have many.

Yes, I entered 2001 yet again in love—but determined to stay grounded and be as good to myself as I was to Doug—and I'd let time reveal if he was "Mr. Right."

In the meantime, we partnered up on a CD. Earth Song would have to do a lot of work to ensure that the CD was excellent and got out there—financial backers, a marketing plan, etc. I definitely understood by then that it would take a lot of capital and a fair amount of time for me to do this right.

At the risk of stating the obvious, it's amazing how much richer life is when one is PRESENT! I'm not saying that after I got clean everything in my life was picture-perfect, but it was all *real*. I was there!—facing stuff, *dealing,* and becoming all the stronger for it. Stronger than before. Strong enough day by day to do better about taking responsibility: for my past, my present—and, yeah, of course, we can't control the future—but I was now much clearer about how my todays might affect my tomorrows. So there I was—she who has no patience for routine—taking on a personal trainer to work on a body I'd neglected for too long.

Okay, I didn't stick with the trainer—but not because I stopped caring about myself. I wanted something that would work my whole self. I settled on yoga. That way I could work simultaneously on my body and my "Soul Power."

Along with my body, I'd also been neglecting my art. After the Purification Program, more and more (and better) drawings flowed. In part, because I started spending more time in the light. I don't know that I'll ever call myself a "morning person," but I've come to delight in waking up in the early morning, as opposed to one, two, or even later in the afternoon as was my habit for years. Being "present" for morning light and morning air is like a mega-vitamin for the soul.

Being "present" also meant not running away from the emotions that overwhelmed me at the Essence Awards in the spring of 2001, and the commitment to tell my story which that moment inspired.

Being "present" meant that when the long-awaited Rufus Reunion wasn't totally smooth sailing (for one, it was interrupted by the horror of 9/11), I was able to take it in stride and think on the positive side. John Robinson, Bobby Watson, Hawk Wolinski, Tony Maiden, Kevin Murphy, and I had finally done something we had talked about doing for years. And through the tour, we gave a lot of people some joy, I felt—from the fans our age longing to relive, for a moment in time, their days of being "Rufusized" to the much, much younger fans who had grown up asking things like, "So, which one is Rufus?"

The tour also gave me occasion to reflect on those long ago days when I was secretly yearning to be a part of Rufus. I had to give thanks. Had Rufus not given me a shot, I might be gigging at some equivalent of Nero's Pit today.

Being "present" also meant that earlier in '01, I was truly able to savor the joy of having another baby in the family: Damien and Dana's girl, Déjà Jade, who was born on my birthday.

It's been two years now of keeping it real. And I just had a birthday of my own. For *months* I had to hear about it.

"The big one's coming up!"

"This is the milestone!"

"We've got to plan something special!"

Since the top of 2003, I had been getting *a lot* of that. But I wasn't feeling my age, feeling ashamed of my age, or fearing my age. The "BIG 5-0" was truly not a big deal to me. (I've never been into earth years, and I've always felt there was a whole lot more wisdom than humor in Satchel Paige's proposition: "How old would you be if you didn't know how old you are?")

Even though I kept telling folks, "It's not a big deal!," there were people in my life who insisted on making a *very* big deal of my fiftieth birthday.

It started on March 20. My Earth Song staff had a little party for me. A beautiful cake!—and I wasn't worrying about the pounds; I was just feeling the love and loving what I was feeling.

The next day, in Detroit, following a gig at the Fox Theatre, my road manager, Simone; my wardrobe person, Elenne (aka El); my back-up singers, my musicians, and the rest of my crew conspired on a surprise party in my hotel suite. A detour to White Castle was part of the ruse.

I had finished my set at the Fox Theatre; Teddy Pendergrass was on stage doing his thing. I was ready to go straight to the car. But El wasn't having any of it.

"Chaka, you need to change out those wet clothes!" (True, I was sweaty after my show.)

So, I obeyed El. And while I was changing I told her that earlier in the day Simone had talked about getting together with a friend of ours who lived in Detroit, and taking in someone else's sound in a club. After my performance, I wasn't feeling up to it. I asked El to let Simone know. All I wanted to do was get back to my hotel room, order up some soup or something, get into my nightgown, watch some tube, go to bed. That's all that was on my mind when Lisa, one of my backup singers, popped into the dressing room.

"Chaka, let's go get some White Castle?"

"Girl, I ain't tryna have no White Castle."

Lisa kept pressing for White Castle and for the crew to then hang out in my room for a bit. "We hardly ever get to spend time with you alone."

"Yeah, come on, Chaka." That was El.

They had a point.

So a bunch of us piled into my limo and headed off for the nearest White Castle. And wouldn't you know it, by then, I had a taste for a fish sandwich or two. By the time we reached a White Castle, thinking about how tiny their sandwiches are, I'd upped the number to four—"And be sure to get A LOT of pickles on the side," I said to the gang that trooped in to get the food.

They were in that White Castle for a millennium! The waiting was making me crazy, so crazy that the next thing I knew I was heading into the place to hurry them up.

As soon as I stepped through the door, the girls behind the counter went off.

"CHAKA KHAN! CHAKA KHAN! CHAKA KHAN!" Then, they started dancing and singing. "WE'RE A GROUP, WE'RE A GROUP!"

In my impatience, I'd forgotten that I wasn't a "regular" person, or at least, I couldn't live like one. Clearly, my presence was causing chaos.

I got my butt back into the limo quick and sent El in to hurry them up. But all she came back with were about six empty white paper bags. The counter girls had begged for autographs.

When Lisa and the others finally emerged with the food—oops! Lisa had eaten two fish sandwiches too many while waiting for the others.

"Girl . . ." I was halfway mad. Between the waiting and my appetite . . . I really *wanted* my four! (Given the dangerous cravings I had for so much of my life, I will not beat myself up over an occasional jones for a fish sandwich—or four!)

When Lisa came back out, she was trailed by one of the counter girls, with a huge, free bag of fish sandwiches.

How beautiful.

I got out of the car and gave the girl a hug, and didn't that set her off. She started dancing—pop-lockin' and stuff.

"You need a dancer, I'm here for you girl, I'm here for you!"

"Alright!" I said as I tucked back into the limo. "Whenever we come back through here we're going to come right here to this White Castle."

I glimpsed in that girl a bit of myself years ago: kind of naïve and nervy at the same time, so eager and high-energy—and getting that first recording contract, cutting that first album was so beyond my wildest dreams that I didn't even dare to dream Grammy.

And there I was in Detroit, facing fifty and nominated for eighteen Grammys. What's more, I had just *won* my eighth Grammy, for a jam with the Funk Brothers on a song from my coming-of-age days: "What's Going On?" I had wanted to do it justice, and I guess I did.

There's no one word for the feeling—ecstasy? relief? joy?—to finally be able to answer that question, to *finally* know what's going on—with me, myself, and I. And that's the start, that's the key. I may not get everything right, but at least I'm getting to know who I am and what I want to be about beyond my singing career.

Back at the hotel—"Happy Birthday to you. . . ."

"Aw, y'all!"

The room ballooned with love: from the gang that had been with me on the White Castle adventure, and from the rest of my crew—musicians, techies.

There was, of course, a big beautiful cake. And what a cornucopia of wonderful gifts!—things they knew I'd use (candles, candleholders, bath stuff) and love (the group gift was a copy of the big, magnificent book *Africa Adorned*).

As much as I had been into "it's not a big deal," the party gave me pause. It's easy to be nonchalant about your birthday and resist the hoopla, but then you stop and think: there are a lot of people out there who have birthdays alone and unremembered, because nobody gives a damn about them. There was no denying it, I was blessed. I couldn't help but tear up as I thought about all the trouble my crew had gone through, from the party fixings and gifts to the stalling at the White Castle.

One of the best gifts I got was humungous basket of fresh tulips—of *every* color on earth! They were a birthday present and a "Welcome to Detroit" gift rolled into one that had been sent to the Fox Theater. The sender was a woman many regard as Detroit's "First Lady," someone I'd emulated as a child and then gotten to know later in life: Aretha. (Our birthdays are two days apart; hers, March 25.)

Appreciating the surprise party and the presents didn't mean I was going to party hearty all night. After some cake and conversation (and no more fish sandwiches), I slipped into my room, had a bath with some of my new goodies, got into my gown, and clicked to the Discovery Channel.

My "real" birthday was coming up that Sunday.

My family had wanted to throw a monster party. "Absolutely not!" I'd said. But I did agree to a simple get-together, and that's what we had at Aunt Kathy's (with her dynamite BBQ chicken and my mother's out-of-this-world ribs).

It was a truly soul-satisfying time: close family, a few close friends, good music in the background, all so beautiful in its simplicity (Talk of Operation Iraqi Freedom was *verboten!*)

Life had, indeed, been so very good to me, much better than I had been to myself for so many years. And how blessed I was to have so much of my family with me still—alive to see me "present" and committed to staying that way.

Gramma Maude, still in L.A.

Aunt Kathy, still being a sister-girlfriend.

Aunt Barbara, still regal and rooted in Chicago.

My father, still living in Berkeley, still listening to jazz. Connie, setting up house in Hawaii.

My sibs were all fine: Bonnie was still in the London house, and still carrying on with her singing career; Mark, who had overcome his problems and long since settled in the Midwest, was helping others overcome theirs as a social worker; Zaheva, was a legal eagle at a top New York law firm; Tammy, was still my trusted personal manager.

My mother was still my business manager, and all our clashing was a thing of the past. That's not to say we won't have our moments. After all, she is a strong-willed woman; I am her strong-willed child. I am her as much as I am my father. But I'm no longer an ingrate.

I realized that however much I may have bucked my mother's authority I never stopped loving her. I realized, too, that, with all her "meddling" she had only been trying to save my life—trying to get me to grow up, get real about responsibilities, especially the responsibility of motherhood. And I did know better. Indeed, I'd had *her*—a mother who was there for me 24/7 and in every emergency, even when I didn't want her to be. I kicked her to the curb, yet she never stopped loving me. I asked her to move to L.A., she upturned her life. I showed out, bugged out, drugged out—she rescued my children. If there were times that she looked at me and thought, *I gave up an Art Institute scholarship for this?* could you blame her? But she never regretted her "Miracle Child." She never gave up on me. Today, time and again I see that so often—most often—Mama knows best. I've come to rely on her wisdom and seek her opinion on many, many matters.

As for my children, Milini was still making her way in music: doing a lot of session work and working on her solo career. And being a better mother to Raeven than I ever was to her.

Damien, Dana, and Déjà were literally living a stone's throw away from me, in the guest house on the property I'd settled on in L.A. after the Purification Program.

Are my grandchildren my "second chance?" Nah. I mean, it's not like Raeven and Déjà don't have good mothers. But what I *can* do now—what I *want* to do now—is be the best grandmother I can be—as strong and "present" for them as Gramma Maude was for me. Raeven and Déjà are a big part of my incentive to remain "present" (and to curb the cussing!)

I don't know how long my birthday party lasted—I left around midnight. Once home, did I meditate or make any resolutions? Nah. I've never been into New Year's or any other red-letter day resolutions; I've never believed in searching for revelations. I simply trust that epiphanies know where to find me. And when. So when I reached home, I just went to sleep.

These days, I have more than enough on my plate—not a lot of space left to get too "future."

Chakawear is on the drawing board (stylish daywear, evening wear, anywhere-wear for us zaftig chicks), with Cousin Dwayne working on development (based on his experience with FUBU).

Also on the launchpad, Chakaroma (scented candles, natural oils, along with creams and other healthy bodycare) and who knows, I might even expand into a line of all-natural remedies. Simone, El, and the rest of my crew call me "Dr. Khan," because whenever they're a little under the weather I'm at the ready with a "prescription" (usually, my apple cider vinegar, honey, and garlic blend.)

At long last, I'm reviving my Chakalates, which I'd launched in the '90s, but hadn't given it the right energy. This time around, I want to do *seriously* better because, like Chakaroma, Chakalates proceeds are earmarked for my foundation. And I want my foundation to get *a lot* of proceeds!

I started the Chaka Khan Foundation in the late '90s, with the mission statement: "To aid and assist women and children at risk. Our vision, to help and educate our society by healing and educating its future leaders, children, and their first teachers, mothers." (It's not that I didn't recognize that there were men in crisis. But truth is truth: women and children are the most victimized members of society.)

Among the ways my foundation has been true to its mission is by donating and raising funds for organizations that do direct rescue work.

How can the homeless possibly get whole without decent shelters and transitional housing?

How can battered women liberate themselves from abuse if they have nowhere safe to go?

How many people are able to get clean and sober without access to quality treatment?

While I'm in no position to open shelters, build affordable housing, or establish a Purification Program-type center right now, I certainly can continue to contribute to organizations that do.

"Reading Is Instrumental," a co-partnership with Rev. Johnson's World Literacy Crusade, is another piece of the Chaka Khan Foundation work. Illiteracy and semi-illiteracy are a sort of slavery—and it's also dangerous. Like all the programs my foundation supports, my involvement with "Reading Is Instrumental" is partially "giving back" and partially just enlightened self-interest.

True, I live a privileged life, but I know the lives of "ordinary" people can affect my life. Think about it: do you shop, call costumer service representatives, go to the dentist, fly? We can't afford to have the people who really keep things going barely literate. Illiterate people can mess up your stuff quick! Too, reading can rescue, be a window onto the world, broaden horizons, turn people into thinkers! And don't you think we need more of those?

Literacy is all the more lifesaving for the poor, especially poor children. Strong reading skills and a passion for books increase the likelihood that a child won't drop out of school, and may even go on to college. Admittedly, that didn't work in my case, but I was fortunate—I was gifted, able to make a great living without a diploma. (And I always had a thirst for knowledge and a passion for reading.) But a success like mine is one-in-a-million. "Making it" in life without an education is a really rare thing.

Along with the importance of literacy, the healing power of visual art remains an interest for me. Through my foundation, I continue to help WLC maintain (and create) Chaka Khan Art Clubs in cities around the nation.

What are you contributing? That's a question that no longer dogs me. Through the fire—of my voice, my personality—I am determined to do more to help others overcome. Such clear and present thinking has triggered another epiphany: that it's about time I devote a piece of my foundation to autism. I might name that component "Tallon's Tower."

I named Tammy's first-born before he was born: "You've *got* to name him Tallon!" (I really dig the legend of King Arthur and The Knights of the Round Table.) Poor Tammy. I wouldn't relent.

Tallon seemed fine until he was about two. He had started walking at a normal time, and was doing quite a bit of talking. Then, after a series of vaccinations, Tallon began to lose language. He seemed to be living in his own world more and more (a lot more than children normally do). Tammy thought it was just a phase.

When Tallon was about three, Aunt Barbara prompted Tammy to rethink that. "You should have him assessed; I think there are some delays."

Like many parents who get painful advice, Tammy was at first offended, upset, and in denial (the ole easier-to-be-mad-than-sad syndrome.) But Tammy didn't stay in denial. She followed Aunt Barbara's advice.

After Tallon was diagnosed as autistic, Tammy and Howard went all-out to get Tallon the best treatment and therapies available (everything from adjusting his diet to occupational and behavioral therapy). Tallon was regaining some speech by 2003.

Tallon is among the more than 1.5 million children in America diagnosed as autistic. Environmental toxins? Vaccines? Genetics? There are all kinds of theories about the cause. But there's no debating the fact that, while scientists are working on cause and cure, we who care about the future need to do some serious work on creating public awareness about autism and support systems for the generations of autistic adults who are with us now and will be until we find a cure.

My foundation is important to me. It's not that I haven't always been a giver. But after I got clean, I wanted to be less careless with my giving. Fortifying and expanding the Chaka Khan Foundation is one of the ways I've been able to work on that.

"Do you feel like your life has come full circle?" asked the interviewer for Lifetime's *Intimate Portraits,* a few weeks before my fiftieth birthday.

I chuckled. That's not a concept I can really get with.

"No, I don't feel my life's come full circle at all," I replied. "I think I've had two circles. I'm working on the third now. I feel like I'm at four o'clock on the third circle."

And when I hit the stroke of midnight—Hell if I know.

I'm not finished yet.

CHAKA!